Nature's Melody

by
Betty L. Benson
for
The Garden Club of Georgia, Inc.

Edited by
Thomas S. Patrick

Photography by
Betty L. Benson

Illustrations by
Alisa Moore

A guide to native wildflowers,
ferns, shrubs, trees and vines
for gardens in the State of Georgia.

Save the "melody" – grow wild!
Betty Benson

Published by
THE GARDEN CLUB OF GEORGIA, INC.
325 S. Lumpkin Street, Athens, GA 30602-1865

Printed in the United States of America
by Columbus Productions, Inc.
Columbus, Georgia
First Printing, 1994

The Cover: *Viguiera porteri* (Stone Mountain Yellow Daisy, Confederate Daisy)
Photographed on the Milner Farm in Pike County, Georgia.

ISBN 0-9612486-0-2

DEDICATION

To my husband, David,
with my love and
sincere appreciation for
his patience, support
and understanding.

TABLE OF CONTENTS

FOREWORD

My earliest childhood memory about flowers goes back to a time when I was under school age. I was playing in the woods behind my grandmother's home in Fulton County. The area is now within the city limits of Atlanta. I found a flower that, even to my young eyes, was beautiful beyond belief. For some reason I did not pick it but instead hurriedly got my aunt to come with me to identify my "find." I was informed that it was a ladyslipper. I do not remember seeing another one for many, many years. I was just as excited the second time as I was the first because I knew what it was then.

My uncle's wife was from the mountains of North Georgia, and she often told me of the beauty of the mountain laurel and rhododendron. When I was about twelve she took me on a visit to Dahlonega where I saw for myself that everything she remembered about them was true. Childhood memories also include woods full of honeysuckle (wild azalea), sweet shrub, dogwood and violets. The sights and smells were wonderful.

The flowers were just always there — every spring. Then they seemed to just disappear and were, you might say, out of sight and out of mind, until 1977 when my husband and I made an automobile trip to the western part of the United States. It was springtime when the wildflowers were truly in their glory. My childhood memories revived, my interest was stimulated and I have been a lover and student of wildflowers ever since. My husband has become almost as enthusiastic about them as I. Our private wildflower garden has over 100 species including the endangered *Hydrastis canadensis* (goldenseal) and the threatened *Cypripedium acaule* (pink ladyslipper) and *Cypripedium calceolus* (yellow ladyslipper).

ACKNOWLEDGEMENTS

It is hard to acknowledge all of those from whom you get assistance when you undertake a project such as writing a book on Georgia wildflowers.

First and foremost I thank my husband, David, for the many things he has done to make my efforts bear fruit.

I thank Deen Day Smith (Mrs. Charles O., Jr.), former president of The Garden Club of Georgia, for encouraging me to undertake such an endeavor.

I am indebted to Marvina Northcutt (Mrs. Guy H., Jr.), and Helen Hargreaves (Mrs. William B.) for permitting me to use the name *Nature's Melody*.

I am deeply grateful to Tom Patrick for spending much time and effort in editing the text and without whose help this book could not have been completed.

I thank Elizabeth Neal (Mrs. Bernard) for use of the photograph of the *Scuttelaria montana* (large-flowered skullcap).

I express my gratitude to the many people who have shared wildflower plants and seeds with me and those who have allowed me to make photographs of plants on their property.

I thank the Georgia Department of Natural Resources for allowing me to use the physiographic map, Georgia's Protected Plant List and for supplying me with a listing of the parks where wildflower trails are maintained.

I thank those persons who work in the many parks and gardens I have visited who maintain the wildflowers and who, in keeping the plants in existence, make an undertaking such as this possible.

I extend my appreciation to every person who has in any way been of assistance. To each and everyone of them I am truly grateful.

— *Betty Benson*

INTRODUCTION

This book is a guide for some of the wildflowers, shrubs, trees, vines, ferns and groundcovers that grow in the State of Georgia. No attempt has been made to identify all native plants. That task would be next to impossible and such an effort would fill volumes.

Both botanical and common names are listed. Scientific or botanical names are given to plants so that they can be readily distinguished from one another and their identities can be communicated from person to person all over the world. Linnaeus, Swedish botanist, devised an arrangement for giving a double name to every plant. This scientific name is usually of Latin or Greek origin. The first name is the genus and is always capitalized. The second name may be written in lower case and identifies the species. Either of the names may be descriptive of the plant's habitat, place of origin, its discoverer or some other identifying characteristic. The botanical name is used and recognized universally. There can be only one correct scientific name for any one plant. Names are sometimes changed to accomodate newly gathered information much to the consternation of gardeners.

A common name is just that — one that is commonly used. It may be adapted from the plant's growth habit or some evident characteristic, usage or folklore. The problem with using common names is that they are not universal. They are not even national. A plant will have a different common name from one area to another, or the same name could be used for an entirely different plant.

Terminology has been kept in layman's language whenever possible. The glossary will assist where it was necessary to use unfamiliar terminology in describing certain parts of the plant.

The name of the plant family, its lifespan and height are given along with a description of the bloom and the leaves. Cultural requirements, habitat and propagation techniques have been specified. If you attempt to grow wild plants, you will find you will have more success if these specifications are duplicated as closely as possible.

PURPOSE

"...Consider the lilies of the field, how they grow; they toil not, neither do they spin; and yet I say unto you, that even Solomon in all his glory was not arrayed like one of these." (Matthew 6:28-29). The "lilies of the field" that Jesus spoke about were no doubt wildflowers. Many of them grew in the Holy Land at the time Jesus was on earth. God adorned them with such majestic beauty that the finest clothing one could make or buy (King Solomon's opulent robes) paled in comparison. That is still true today.

This great country was once filled with many wild plants — plants of all sizes and descriptions that grew unaided by the hand of man. However, man and man alone has contributed greatly to the demise of these wildings. The plants have been picked, pulled up, polluted, cut down, bulldozed and burned. Their habitats have been destroyed, paved over and built up. Some no longer have the conditions they require to grow. Some are now extinct. Others are rare, endangered or threatened. More will become so unless a concentrated effort is made to preserve what is left.

We all need to learn to recognize, appreciate, conserve and grow wild plants. Conservation and cultivation of these plants is a must if future generations are to know and enjoy them. If a plant becomes extinct, nothing that human beings can do will rectify that situation. The miracle of the seed is God's miracle. Only He can make a tree and only He can make a wildflower.

I hope that this book will be useful in the identification, conservation and cultivation of our native plants, in particular, those known to grow in Georgia. The plants described, though not all true natives, will grow in most areas of the state.

GEORGIA — LAND OF DIVERSITY

Georgia, located in the southeastern United States, is made up of 58,876 square miles — 315 miles long and 250 miles wide. It has over 23 million acres of woodland, generously sprinkled with some of the country's richest flora.

Georgia is a land of vast geological differences and provides within her boundaries the habitats needed by many kinds of wild plants. It has been divided into five physiographic areas:

Cumberland Plateau: extreme northwest Georgia — an elevated tract of flat or sloping land with sandstone bluffs in the southernmost part of the Appalachian Mountains.

Ridge and Valley: extends from Alabama eastward along the south lines of Polk and Bartow Counties and then north just inside the eastern side of Bartow, Gordon and Murray County lines to Tennessee. The terrain is made up of mountain ridges, slopes and limestone valleys with elevations ranging from 500 to 2,000 feet above sea level.

Blue Ridge: runs on a diagonal line that extends northeastward from the extreme northwest corner of Cherokee County to the south line of Rabun County in extreme northeast Georgia. This area composes the southeastern terminus of the Blue Ridge Mountains and contains several mountains higher than 4,000 feet. Brasstown Bald at 4,784 feet above sea level is the highest elevation in the state.

Piedmont: area south of the above regions and north of the Coastal Plain. It is made up of foothills in the north to a few scattered and isolated mountains, the southernmost mountains in the eastern United States in the south. Areas of granite flatrock are among the unique features of the Piedmont.

Coastal Plain: south of a line generally diagonal from the northern boundary of Muscogee County and the Alabama line on the west to the northern boundary of Richmond County and South Carolina on the east. This area is made up of sand hills, flat woods, bays, limestone sinks, bogs and swamps, including the Okefenokee. It also includes the Golden Isles and the Atlantic coastline. The region averages 250 feet above sea level.

The four seasons are easily distinguishable. Spring comes early and is usually short and blustery. The summers are warm and humid but can be very hot. Autumns are mild and sunny. Winters are usually short and mild but there are days of extreme cold. It is always cooler in the mountainous areas. There is a

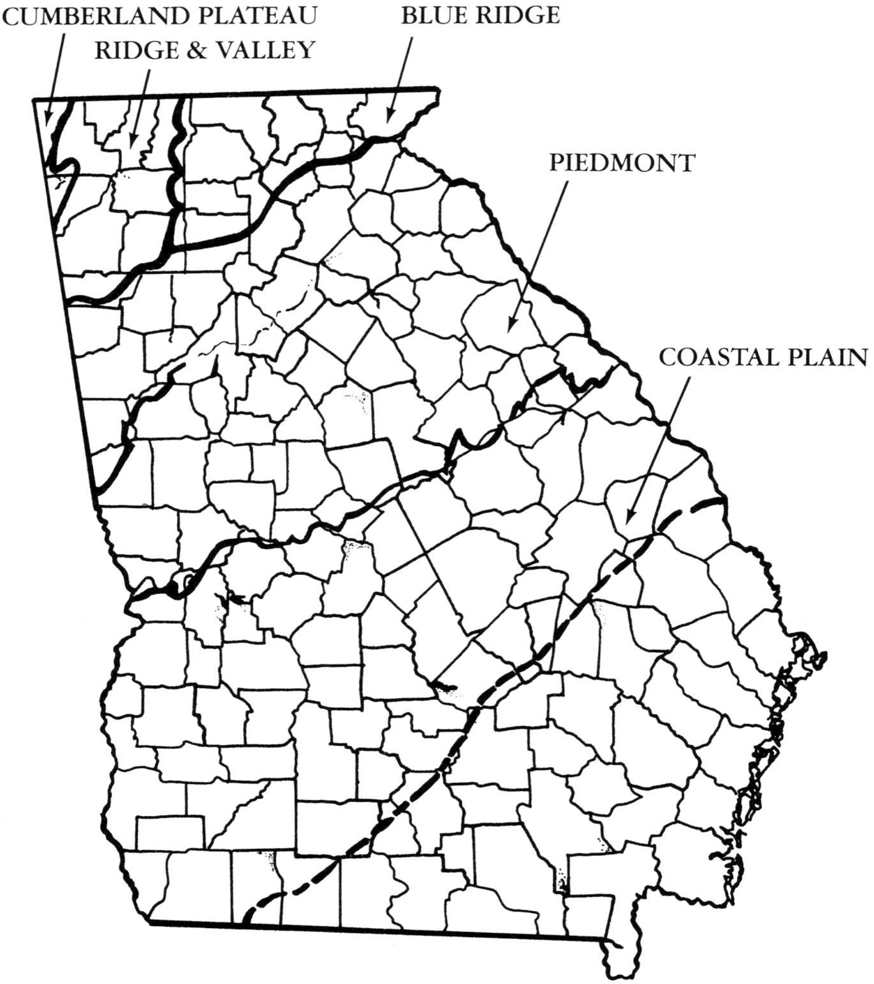

Map courtesy Georgia Department of Natural Resources

wide temperature range – generally from 0 to 100 degrees but the warm days far outnumber the cold.

The annual rainfall average is 75 inches in the northeast Georgia mountains, 49 inches in the Atlanta area (in the Piedmont region) and 42 inches in the east and central areas.

Soil conditions vary from area to area. You will find rich humus soil, red clay, sand, rocky outcroppings and, in some instances, soil that is very poor because of neglect, erosion or overplanting.

With a wide diversity in elevation, vegetation, soil conditions, temperature and rainfall there is an equally wide diversity of wildflowers and other wild plants that are native or that have become acclimated. There is a continuous and wonderous array of these flowers of the wayside and woodlands from February to November.

ENDANGERED, RARE AND THREATENED SPECIES

There are 103 species of wildflowers on the protected list in Georgia. A state plant inventory is currently being conducted by the Georgia Department of Natural Resources and The Nature Conservancy. Some plants not previously known in Georgia have been discovered. Some that were thought to be extinct have been relocated. On bluffs above the Ocmulgee River near Macon a two-foot high woodland plant with blue flowers, the Ocmulgee skullcap, was found. It had been listed as extinct in the mid-1970s by the Smithsonian Institution. The white-petaled bent trillium (*Trillium flexipes*) was found growing on mountain slopes in Walker County.

These and other plants have been added to the official Endangered and Threatened Species list. Three other plants were added to the list. The green pitcher plant (*Sarracenia oreophila*) is a bog plant found only in Towns County in northeast Georgia. The University of Georgia scientists are studying ways to propagate it through both seeds and tissue culture. The pondberry (*Lindera melissifolia*) grows only in Wheeler and Baker Counties in South Georgia. The small-whorled pogonia (*Isotria medeoloides*), a member of the orchid family, has yellow green flowers and dusky green foliage. It was once believed extinct but it has been relocated in North Georgia. It is hoped that the inventory will discover a Franklin tree (*Franklinia altamaha*) the now extinct (in the wild) shrub discovered by William Bartram on the banks of the Altamaha River near old Fort Barrington.

The current protected list includes:

GEORGIA'S PROTECTED PLANTS

1. *Allium speculae* (Flatrock Onion)
2. *Amphianthus pusillus* (Pool Sprite)
3. *Arabis georgiana* (Georgia Rockcress)
4. *Asplenium heteroresiliens* (Spleenwort)
5. *Balduina atropurpurea* (Purple Honeycomb Head)
6. *Baptisia arachnifera* (Hairy Rattleweed)
7. *Bumelia thornei* (Swamp Buckthorn)
8. *Cacalia diversifolia* (Indian Plantain)
9. *Calamintha ashei* (Ohoopee Wild Basil)
10. *Carex baltzellii* (Baltzell Sedge)
11. *Carex biltmoreana* (Biltmore Sedge)
12. *Carex dasycarpa* (Velvet Sedge)
13. *Carex manhartii* (Manhart Sedge)
14. *Carex misera* (Wretched Sedge)

15. *Carex purpurifera* (Purple Sedge)
16. *Ceratiola ericoides* (Rosemary)
17. *Chamaecyparis thyoides* (Atlantic White-cedar)
18. *Chrysopsis pinifolia* (Sandhill Goldenaster)
19. *Croomia pauciflora* (Croomia)
20. *Cuscuta harperi* (Harper Dodder)
21. *Cymophyllus fraseri* (Fraser Sedge)
22. *Cypripedium acaule* (Pink Ladyslipper)
23. *Cypripedium calceolus* (Yellow Ladyslipper)
24. *Draba aprica* (Granite Whitlow-wort)
25. *Echinacea laevigata* (Smooth Purple Coneflower)
26. *Elliottia racemosa* (Georgia Plume)
27. *Epidendrum conopseum* (Greenfly Orchid)
28. *Evolvulus sericeus* (Silky Morning-glory)
29. *Fimbristylis perpusilla* (Harper Fimbristylis)
30. *Fothergilla gardenii* (Dwarf Witch-alder)
31. *Gentianopsis crinita* (Fringed Gentian)
32. *Hartwrightia floridana* (Hartwrightia)
33. *Helonias bullata* (Swamp Pink)
34. *Hexastylis shuttleworthii v. harperi* (Harper Wild Ginger)
35. *Hydrastis canadensis* (Goldenseal)
36. *Hymenocallis coronaria* (Shoals Spiderlily)
37. *Illicium floridanum* (Florida Anise)
38. *Isoetes melanospora* (Black-spored Quillwort)
39. *Isoetes tegetiformans* (Mat-forming Quillwort)
40. *Isotria medeoloides* (Small Whorled Pogonia)
41. *Jeffersonia diphylla* (Twinleaf)
42. *Leavenworthia exigua* (Least Gladecress)
43. *Lindera melissifolia* (Pondberry)
44. *Lindermia saxicola* (False Pimpernel)
45. *Litsea aestivalis* (Pondspice)
46. *Lysimachia fraseri* (Fraser Loosestrife)
47. *Lythrum curtissii* (Curtiss Loosestrife)
48. *Marshallia mohrii* (Coosa Barbara Buttons)
49. *Marshallia ramosai* (Pineland Barbara Buttons)
50. *Matelea alabamensis* (Alabama Milkvine)
51. *Matelea pubiflora* (Trailing Milkvine)
52. *Myriophyllum laxum* (Lax Water-milfoil)
53. *Nestronia umbellula* (Indian Olive)

54. *Neviusia alabamensis* (Alabama Snow-wreath)
55. *Oxypolis canbyi* (Canby Dropwort)
56. *Panicum hirstii* (Panic Grass)
57. *Penstemon dissectus* (Cutleaf Beardtongue)
58. *Physostegia leptophylla* (Narrowleaf Obedient Plant)
59. *Pinguicula primuliflora* (Clearwater Butterwort)
60. *Platanthera integrelabia* (Monkeyface Orchid)
61. *Potentilla tridentata* (Three-tooth Cinquefoil)
62. *Ptilimnium nodosom* (Harperella)
63. *Quercus oglethorpensis* (Oglethorpe Oak)
64. *Rhododendron prunifolium* (Plumleaf Azalea)
65. *Rhus michauxii* (Dwarf Sumac)
66. *Sabatia capitata* (Cumberland Rose Gentian)
67. *Sageretia minutiflora* (Climbing Buckthorn)
68. *Sagittaria secundifolia* (Kral Water-plantain)
69. *Salix floridana* (Florida Willow)
70. *Sanquisorba canadensis* (Canada Burnet)
71. *Sarracenia flava* (Yellow Flytrap)
72. *Sarracenia leucophylla* (Whitetop Pitcherplant)
73. *Sarracenia minor* (Hooded Pitcherplant)
74. *Sarracenia oreophila* (Green Pitcherplant)
75. *Sarracenia psittacina* (Parrot Pitcherplant)
76. *Sarracenia purpurea* (Purple Pitcherplant)
77. *Sarracenia rubra* (Sweet Pitcherplant)
78. *Schisandra glabra* (Bay Starvine)
79. *Schwalbea americana* (Chaffseed)
80. *Scutellaria montana* (Large-flowered Skullcap)
81. *Scutellaria ocmulgee* (Ocmulgee Skullcap)
82. *Sedum nevii* (Nevius Stonecrop)
83. *Sedum pusillum* (Granite Stonecrop)
84. *Senecio millefolium* (Blue Ridge Ragwort)
85. *Shortia galacifolia* (Oconee-bells)
86. *Silene polypetala* (Fringed Campion)
87. *Silene regia* (Royal Catchfly)
88. *Spiraea virginiana* (Virginia Spirea)
89. *Spiranthes magnicamporum* (Great Plains Ladies-tresses)
90. *Stewartia malacodendron* (Silky Camellia)
91. *Stylisma pickeringii var. pickeringii* (Pickering Morningglory)
92. *Thalictrum cooleyi* (Cooley Meadowrue)

93. *Thalictrum debile* (Trailing Meadowrue)
94. *Tillandsia recurvata* (Ball-moss)
95. *Torreya taxifolia* (Florida Torreya)
96. *Trientalis borealis* (Starflower)
97. *Trillium persistens* (Persistent Trillium)
98. *Trillium reliquum* (Relict Trillium)
99. *Veratrum woodii* (Ozark Bunchflower)
100. *Viburnum bracteatum* (Limerock Arrowwood)
101. *Waldsteinia lobata* (Piedmont Barren Strawberry)
102. *Xerophyllum asphodeloides* (Eastern Turkeybeard)
103. *Xyris tennesseensis* (Tennessee Yellow-eyed Grass)

Descriptions and pictures of the majority of these endangered and threatened plants are not included in this book. A detailed listing and description has been incorporated into a loose-leaf book entitled "Georgia's Protected Plants" by Jerry L. McCollum and David R. Ettman of the Georgia Department of Natural Resources and is available from the department upon request.

Do not pick or dig these plants from public lands! Leave them to multiply in their natural setting.

Conservation is more than not doing something. It is actively doing something. Learn about wildflowers and learn about those on this list.

Watch for construction sites and roadway development. Any plants growing in that environment are in danger of destruction. It is better to move plants when they are dormant. If time permits, clearly mark the plant when it is in bloom and move it when it is dormant. If, however, it is in the path of danger and imminent destruction, it should be moved immediately. Always get permission to move plants from the owner of the property. When plants are moved always be sure to move them to a properly suited and maintained area.

BEAUTIFICATION PROJECTS

Many wildflowers and other native plants have been destroyed by the development of the interstate highway system as well as by state highway development. As a result of such destruction, "Operation Wildflower" was adopted and copyrighted by the National Council of State Garden Clubs, Inc. It is a national effort to beautify roadsides and to educate the public in the appreciation, preservation and propagation of native wildflowers and other native plants. Its aim is to restore and conserve the wildflowers and to beautify the roadsides along the nation's highways. In 1987 Federal Highway legislation made native wildflowers, seeds or seedlings, a part of any landscaping project.

In an attempt to help cut down on litter on the state's highways and to add to the beauty of the roadsides, The Garden Club of Georgia, Inc., and the Georgia Department of Transportation began a program to promote the increase of wildflowers on the highway right-of-ways in 1974. Perpetual funding for this program was made available in 1979. Hundreds of miles of roadsides have been planted with wildflowers, not only beautifying the areas but saving mowing costs, personnel services and equipment costs.

The Parks and Public Lands Beautification Incentive Program, a cooperative effort between The Garden Club of Georgia, Inc., and the Georgia Department of Natural Resources, was launched in the spring of 1987. Its aim is to beautify and improve a part of the 60,000 acres of state-owned land and to encourage the use of native plants in landscaping. It was designed to encourage park employees to plan and implement projects to beautify, enhance and conserve the natural beauty of 43 State parks and 14 historic sites operated by the Georgia Department of Natural Resources. This program was modeled after the Georgia Highway Wildflower Program. Perpetual funding has been provided for this program. There are four categories of beautification: Conservation and Reclamation, Wildflower Meadow Gardening, Beauty Spots and Extended Project Maintenance. The purpose of Conservation and Reclamation is to reclaim overused sites or to conserve areas that have a high incident of erosion or compaction. Native trees, shrubs, plants and groundcovers and grasses are the plants of choice. Wildflower Meadow Gardening covers the planting of wildflowers and other low maintenance groundcovers on no less than one-half acre. Beauty Spots emphasizes planting in highly visible areas. The use of native plants is preferred. Extended Project Maintenance is used to encourage continued maintenance of quality projects that have been entered in previous years.

Information concerning either of these programs may be obtained by writing The Garden Club of Georgia, Inc., 325 South Lumpkin Street, Athens, Georgia, 30602.

GARDENING WITH WILD PLANTS

A wild plant is any plant that grows naturally in the wild – woods, roadsides, fields, prairies, mountains, marshes, bogs or desert. Escapes or aliens are those plants that were not originally native to the United States. They were introduced as garden plants or came to the country via some other manner and have escaped from cultivation. Several of these garden escapes are well established, persist in the wild and are truly naturalized. To call them other than wild seems almost foolish.

Many families comprise the makeup of wild plants. There is a vast range in shape, size, color, arrangement and pattern of the flower and of the leaves. The bloom period starts in late February or early March and usually ends with frost. Some shrubs even bloom in winter.

Any area that supports greenery can be adapted for wild plants. A woodland garden is a place for growing woodland wild plants in a place similar to their native habitat. Wild plants also grow in meadows, fields or any other locality that suits their cultural requirements.

It is not necessary that you have a nature preserve or lots of acreage to grow wildflowers and other wild plants. All you need is either a shady spot or a meadowlike area in your yard.

You will have to learn to take a different approach to your concept of gardening. In addition to studying books for instructions on how to grow different kinds of plants, study the way they grow in nature. That is your best guideline. Native plants are exacting in their requirements, so compatible conditions must be provided. The natural conditions in your yard, including the soil type, pH, fertility, drainage, light and sun must be considered for each type of plant. In addition before you plant any wildflower, be sure that the plant is recommended for your area. To plant outside the required environment will likely be futile as growth will probably be poor, and it is possible the plant will die. Try to grow only those flowers which like the conditions you have or which you can adapt for the flowers.

Test the soil consistency to see if it is suitable. Dig a hole six inches deep (you need at least four inches of top soil for woodland flowers), moisten a handful of soil and squeeze. The most desirable soil, one rich in leaf mold and decayed vegetable matter, separates into several large lumps. If the soil is heavy or light, modify it by the addition of humus.

In planning a wildflower garden you need to first analyze your property and decide what sort of garden you want. Study existing vegetation, land slopes, and protruding rocks. Growth will be on several levels – trees (tall and short), shrubs, flowers and ferns (tall and short), vines and ground covers. A good wildflower garden combines several of these for variety and scale to make it more interesting.

Your objective is to have an attractive year-round display. Plan and plant for blooms and berries in the spring, summer, and fall. You should have a variety of shapes and textures. The best source of foliage is ferns. With them you can achieve a cool and pleasing effect.

Wildflowers will not thrive in compacted soil and must be planted where they will not be walked on, even in the winter. Plan access paths so you can easily reach the beds for planting, mulching, other tasks and for viewing. Paths should always appear as natural as possible so when you add rocks, be sure they are weathered in order to create a natural scene. Wild plants of the same type usually grow in clusters instead of neat rows. Allow them to spread. They are happier when left completely undisturbed. They might even move to a spot they like better.

COLLECTING SEED

You will find that you can grow wildflowers year after year from your own seed. They have been producing seed for years and will continue to do so unless they are hindered by man. Most reproduce themselves readily.

Types of seed are as varied as types of plants. Some are very small, and some have tufts and are dispersed by the wind. Others are large and heavy, making good food for the birds. Some are woody capsules that contain many small, hard seed. Some are as thin as wafers, and some are borne inside berries or a pulp.

You can collect seed from your own garden, of course, but you can also make notations as to other places when flowers are blooming. Select healthy blooms when picking seed. Mark the plant before the seed ripens and make a note of where it is growing — the name of the road, on which side, some permanent identifying marker, whether on a bank, in a ditch, or on a rock. Be sure that you collect only mature seed and that you always leave enough for natural propagation where they are growing. You do not want to contribute to the demise of any plant.

Observe conditions carefully. Study plant habits to learn when seeds mature and the qualities indicating ripeness that will be evident. Capsules or pods usually enlarge and change color before they ripen. This will vary on different plants. Annuals and biennials can bear seed a month or so after blooming. After their second year perennials will need to be watched carefully for the proper time to gather the seed. Some mature and drop seed rapidly and must be inspected daily or wrapped with nylon netting or stocking to catch seed. The longer you leave the seed, the greater your risk of losing it to the wind, rain, birds or to its own exploding mechanism if it is a plant which disperses its seeds to great distances when it opens. Choose a day that is dry and a time when the plant is not wet with dew or rain. Tie the netting or stocking around the seed capsule lightly to keep the seed from being dispersed or eaten. When ripe cut the seed head from the plant and store it until the seed pod has dried out and is ready to release its seed. In dry areas store seed in a paper bag so air can pass through it. When the seeds are ripe and dry shake out, remove all debris and either sow immediately or put in an airtight container and store in the refrigerator. Keeping seed cold will help them last longer. It is necessary that some seed be scarified or stratified (see glossary). Seeds that have fleshy fruits or pulp must be cleaned as they have a tendency to rot if left in their natural state. Never store seed in plastic until they are absolutely dry. In damp areas, store the completely dried seed in moisture proof jars with the lid securely fastened.

Label all seeds as to what they are (common and botanical names), when and where collected. *Never* collect seed from plants on the endangered or threatened species list. *Never* collect seed on another person's property without getting permission.

In collecting seed you will need, in addition to knowledge about the plant, guesswork and luck, but usually your results will be well worth the effort.

VEGETATIVE REPRODUCTION

The purpose of vegetative reproduction, in addition to increasing your stock of plants, is to insure exact genetic reproduction (you get a plant that will resemble its parent in every way) and to obtain plants more quickly than growing from seed. To grow from seed can sometimes take years on certain plants.

Cuttings may be taken from softwood growth, hardwood growth or from roots. The leaf may be used in some instances. Plants may also be divided or layered.

Stem Cuttings

Take the cuttings when the plant is in active growth, generally from June to August. Softwood cuttings should be taken from the plant tissue that is half ripened. This method is especially good for herbaceous perennials such as geraniums, lupines, and beardtongue. The plant should be well watered, healthy and in good condition (free of disease and insects). It is best to take cuttings on an overcast day. Take cuttings from the tips of the longer shoots or from sideshoots, making the cut just below a leaf or node, using a good sharp tool. The cutting should be 3 - 5 inches long. Use stems where the leaves are close together. Leave the cut on the mother plant just above a node or leaf but do not leave a stem above the remaining leaf. Remove any buds from the cutting. Pinch off the lower 2 - 3 sets of leaves. Do not rip them off as this will tear the plant tissue. It is from this part of the stem that the root will emerge.

If you are not able to plant the cutting immediately, put it in water to keep it from wilting, making sure that it is correctly identified. When ready to plant, dip the cutting in water (preferably containing a fungicide) and then dip the cutting in a rooting hormone to induce and stimulate the production of roots. Be sure 2 - 3 nodes are covered with the rooting powder. Rooting powder comes in several concentrations, easy, medium, hard. Select according to the rooting requirements of the cutting you are attempting to root. It is best to put some of the rooting powder in a separate shallow container or on paper. Do not dip the cutting into the package containing all of the rooting hormone. To do so might spread disease and would wet the remaining powder. Do not dislodge the rooting hormone when inserting the cutting into the rooting medium.

Root Cuttings

This method of vegetative reproduction is good for increasing plants that have a thick or creeping rootstock like butterfly weed, asters, bleeding heart or yucca. Take when dormant (usually in winter or late fall when the leaves have dropped). Mark the locale of the plant when it is in bloom so it will be easily found. Always make sure you dig deep enough to get all of the root system. Lift the plant, wash off the roots and cut off the tops. Cut off all air roots. Separate the roots if necessary. Make slanted cuts. Sections to be rooted should be 2 - 3 inches long. Dust with a fungicide. The top of the root should always point upward so the top should be identified in some manner. Plant in the medium with the top side up (not flat) with the top of the cutting at or just below the surface of the medium. Water in and keep moist. When the new shoots appear, protect from full sun. When new growth is sufficient, transplant and keep watered well. Keep the rooting shaded until it is established.

Potting Medium For Cuttings

Whether you are using stem or root cuttings you should use a good rooting medium preferably 1/2 peat and 1/2 perlite (or sand, etc). Pure soil is too heavy to encourage quick root development. Smooth the surface of the rooting medium and tamp down gently. The medium should be moist. Plant the cutting so 2 - 3 nodes are covered with soil. Water thoroughly to make certain all air pockets are closed. It is very important that cuttings have good drainage. Cuttings should never be allowed to wilt. Sprinkle or spray frequently, especially on hot days. Sufficient moisture can be maintained by using a hand mister or enclosing in a plastic bag or cold frame. Keep cuttings out of direct sunlight until roots have developed.

When transplanting seedlings or rooted cuttings, water with a solution containing a transplanting liquid to help encourage further root development and to retard transplant shock. These transplant liquids can be purchased from your nursery. Keep plants shaded until they become acclimated.

Division

Plants should be divided when they become crowded and when they are not in active growth. Most plants should be divided while they are dormant (late fall, winter or before new growth starts in the spring). Always leave enough time for the plant roots to become re-established before heaving of the ground by freezing. Dig the plant, shake off the soil and rinse the roots. If the plant has a bushy growth, most of the top foliage should be removed. Look for a place within the root system that has a natural division and gently tease or cut apart with a sharp knife. Hard clumps may have to be pried apart with two spading forks or cut apart with a spade that is flat on the bottom. Reset the separated sections at the same depth at which they originally grew. Water with a solution containing transplant liquid to help reduce shock. Shield from direct sun and keep watered until established.

TRANSPLANTING

Many wildflowers can be successfully transplanted. The best time to move them is just after their flowering season is over but before they die down and disappear. Dig each plant carefully getting as much soil as possible. Lift the plant into a previously prepared container for transporting. Most shrubs should be pruned severely to match the root system in size. Never let the root system dry out. The plant should be transplanted to its new location as soon as possible. Set it at the same depth it was when in its natural location, press the soil gently but firmly around the roots and water well to settle the soil and prevent air pockets. Shade the transplant for a few days. Keep watered until wilting ceases and the plant appears to be adapted. Always keep watered during dry seasons.

SEED GERMINATION

In addition to the right soil, seed germination requires the right conditions of temperature, moisture, light and air. Different types of seed have different requirements to germinate. The majority require darkness to germinate and must be covered with soil. A few require light to germinate and should not be covered with soil. Some need special treatment (stratification or scarification). Some need to be sown in the fall as they must go through a cold period before they will germinate. Native and naturalized plant seeds fit into all categories.

If no species name is given in the following list, there are two or more varieties of the genus.

Seeds That Need Light to Germinate

Botanical Name	Common Name
Achillea millefolium	yarrow
Aquilegia canadensis	columbine
Penstemon	beardtongue
Hesperis matronalis	dame's rocket

Seeds That Require Cold, Scarification and/or Stratification To Germinate

Botanical Name	Common Name
Actaea pachypoda	baneberry, doll's eyes (remove pulp)
Aquilegia canadensis	columbine
Arisaema dracontium	green dragon (remove pulp)
Arisaema triphyllum	jack-in-the pulpit (remove pulp)
Asclepias tuberosa	butterfly weed
Aster novae-angliae	New England aster
Belamcanda chinensis	blackberry lily (remove pulp)
Campsis radicans	trumpet vine
Castilleja coccinea	Indian paint brush
Clematis virginiana	virgin's bower
Clintonia	bluebead lily, wood lily (remove pulp)
Dicentra cucullaria	dutchman's breeches
Dicentra eximia	bleeding heart
Dodecatheon meadia	shooting star
Echinacea purpurea	purple coneflower
Epigaea repens	trailing arbutus (remove pulp)
Eupatorium	Joe Pye weed
Gaillardia	Indian blanket
Gentiana	gentian
Geranium maculatum	wild geranium
Halesia carolina	silverbell
Houstonia caerulea	bluet
Iris	iris
Lathyrus latifolius	everlasting pea, sweetpea
Liatris	dense blazing star
Lilium superbum	turk's cap lily
Lupinus perennis	wild lupine
Mertensia virginica	Virginia bluebells

Mitchella repens	partridge berry (remove pulp)
Penstemon	beardtongue
Phlox paniculata	garden phlox
Podophyllum peltatum	mayapple (remove pulp)
Polygonatum biflorum	Solomon's seal (remove pulp)
Rosa carolina	Carolina rose (remove pulp)
Sanguinaria canadensis	bloodroot
Sisyrinchium angustifolium	blue eyed grass
Smilacina racemosa	false Solomon's seal (remove pulp)
Tiarella cordifolia	foam flower
Trillium	trillium, toadshade, wake robin
Uvularia	merry bells, bellwort
Vernonia noveboracensis	New York ironweed
Viburnum	witch hobble, arrowwood
Viola	violets
Wisteria	wisteria

MEADOW GARDENING

A meadow garden is a sunny area planted with wildflowers. Choose flowers that will be compatible with one another and that thrive in your area and in your soil. Choose plants with a diversity of color, texture and shape but try to plant species that grow together naturally. Plan for all season color so select plants that will bloom in the spring, summer, and fall.

Your garden can be large or small. It should have a natural appearance, not a formal look. Determine your growing conditions — moisture and light available, soil type, pH. Choose plants that will grow under the conditions you have. Emulate nature as closely as possible.

If you order wildflower seeds, read the package label carefully and follow instructions. If you are planting seed gathered from the wild, select a good book and read what you should do.

Be patient. It takes time to establish and maintain a good meadow garden. Annuals will bloom the first year, biennials the second. It may take longer to get a good stand of perennials but once you have them, they are likely to last for a long time. Some authorities prefer fall planting as it usually produces a better stand of flowers the first year.

Soil Preparation

Start with a clean seedbed. Remove as much vegetation as possible by rototilling, digging, or handweeding often. When the area is clear of weeds, incorporate weedfree manures, compost, or peat to help retain moisture and to improve the soil. Apply a balanced fertilizer lightly and incorporate well into the soil with a rototiller. It is not necessary to dig deep. Water and wait for the flush of weeds. Pull them up, rototill or hoe to kill the weed seedlings. It is very important that you do this first or the weed seedlings will outgrow and smother your wildflower seedlings.

After the flush of weeds have been removed sow the wildflower seed. Rake after sowing to create a level seed bed and to compact the soil sufficiently.

Seeding

Sow according to directions. Usually seeds germinate only when the soil temperature is high enough. For this reason it is probably better to wait until after the last frost except for those seed that require cold or some other special treatment for germination. Mix the seed with wet sand or rotted sawdust. Do not sow on a windy day as the wind will scatter the seed and dry them out. Go over the entire area twice in a crisscross fashion. Rake the seed in about 1/4 inch deep. Note: Some seed require *light* for germination. These seed are *not* to be covered, so toss them on the seedbed after you have raked in the others.

Mulch

Mulch provides protection for emerging roots and shoots by giving both shade and reducing evaporation. Pine straw makes a good mulch and is weed free. Water the seed through the mulch.

Watering

Water at least twice a day, (three or four times a day on hot or windy days) – for about three weeks. Keep the surface damp so that seedlings do not dry out. *Do not* saturate as this could result in dampening off and cause death of the seedlings. When the seedlings appear, water once a day when needed. Usually after about five or six weeks you can water twice a week, tapering off to once a week. When plants become established they will need to be watered only during dry seasons.

Weeds

Remove weeds by hand before they become established. *Do not* use a weedkiller as it will kill the wildflowers.

Mowing

Cut in the late summer or fall to prevent weed seeds and to scatter flower seed for another season of bloom

THE WOODLAND GARDEN

Most woodland wildflowers bloom in the early spring when there is more water and sunlight in the woods. Many of them bloom before the leaves fully develop. They are then protected from the heat by the shade when the leaves are mature. Woods offer the plants both nutrients and the protection they need in order to survive.

An area in your yard that has trees, either coniferous and/or deciduous, can be used as a site for a woodland garden. Your aim is to duplicate the natural habitat in terms of soil, moisture and light so that it is similar to that preferred by the plants you attempt to grow.

Do not completely clear the area but do remove weedy undergrowth and tangled masses. You should have clearly defined paths as wildflowers do not like to be stepped on even when they are dormant. Make the garden as naturalistic and attractive as possible.

The soil should be rich in humus. You should add compost, manure, and well-rotted leaf mold to increase humus. To adequately prepare the soil, dig to a depth of eight to ten inches and cover with loose organic material that will readily decompose into humus.

Woodland wildflowers require no cultivation and should be carefully weeded by hand. Many of them have shallow roots that are easily injured. To damage the root system is to damage and set back the plant.

Wildflowers should not be chemically fertilized. In the fall mulch the garden with crushed leaves to protect the plants, to conserve moisture and to give them an ample and constant supply of the nutrients they like best. Mulching will also help prevent weeds during the active growth period.

Weed-killing chemicals will kill the wildflowers along with the weeds. Do not use them.

BEES, BIRDS AND BUTTERFLIES

A garden of wildflowers, native vines, shrubs and trees is an open invitation to other wild things — bees, birds and butterflies. The number and kinds of bees, birds and butterflies that you attract depends on what you plant and the surrounding vegetation in your area. They are all attracted by a profusion of brightly colored nectar producing flowers.

Bees and Pollination

The role of the couriers, bees and butterflies, who carry the pollen from one flower to another is the most fabulous role in all nature. Without pollination the world would be without seed, without food, without flowers. Some flowers have pollen that is too heavy to be transported by the wind, and it must be transported in some other manner.

In order for the flower to attract the insects that pollinate it, the flowers must have a special color or odor. The insect is directed to the flower center, the nectar, and the reproductive organs. Flowers pollinated by the honeybees, butterflies and other insects are usually colorful and showy.

Honeybees are the most important of all insects in carrying pollen. While gathering nectar from the flowers honeybees also collect pollen in special pollen baskets and on their hind legs. As they fly from flower to flower some of the pollen collected from one flower will rub off on the next flower they visit. This is pollination, and it has to occur before a flower can produce seeds. Seeds are needed to produce new plants. A lot of flowers are totally dependent on the honeybee for pollination.

NECTAR PRODUCING WILDFLOWERS

ageratum	Joe Pye weed
beardtongue	lobelia
black eyed susan	lupine
blanket flower	mallow
blazing star	meadow sweet
blueberry	milkweed
boneset	monarda
bugle	New England aster
bur marigold	ox-eye daisy
butterfly weed	phlox
coreopsis	purple coneflower
cornflower	Queen Anne's lace
cosmos	sunflower
dandelion	thrift
goldenrod	touch me not
ironweed	yarrow

Butterflies

Butterflies have been called "flying gems" and "winged flowers." Some are skittish while others flutter and flit from flower to flower. They come in a variety of colors, shapes and patterns. In addition to their beauty they are second only to the honeybee in the pollination of plants. Propagation of flowers, fruits, and vegetables is assured through pollen carried by the butterfly.

Habitat loss is the greatest enemy for butterflies. Plant a butterfly wildflower garden and practice butterfly watching in your own yard. Butterfly watching can be shared with children and with friends.

You can do six things to attract butterflies to your garden:

1. Have sunny, open areas planted to provide a continuous source of food.
2. Provide a nearby water source.
3. Plant nectar-rich flowers. Bright, flat-topped flowers are most suitable.
4. Plant host plants on which they can lay their eggs and which will provide food for the larvae. Each butterfly species has a favorite food plant on which it lays its eggs.
5. Provide protected places for the larvae to pupate. Different species require different conditions. The pupal stage can last from eight to ten days to more than a year. Tall grasses and foliage provide safe resting spots.
6. Use no insecticides in the butterfly garden.

The female deposits her tiny eggs either on the leaves, stalk, or flower of the host plant, the plant on which the larvae will feed. The very minute young will begin eating immediately and voraciously and will continue to do so for about two weeks. Providing favorite plants for food will help prevent them from eating other garden plants. Toward the end of summer the larvae spin a cocoon in which to hibernate through the winter.

How to recognize a butterfly as opposed to a moth:

1. When at rest they fold their wings over their heads.
2. They fly during the daylight hours.
3. They have knobs on their slender antennae.
4. They are slender bodied.
5. Their patterns are repetitive and geometric.
6. They have vivid colors.

Several butterflies populate areas of Georgia. Among them are the brushfoot butterflies which are medium sized and generally some shade of orange. This group includes admirals, fritallaries, crescentspots, angelwings and painted ladies. The swallowtails are large and brightly colored and have tailed hind wings. The gossamer wings include the hairstreaks which are usually tailed. The milkweed butterflies are usually orange with black margins.

Butterfly	Host Plant	Nectar Source
Brushfoot		
American painted lady	everlasting, pearly everlasting	
Baltimore	turtlehead, foxglove, plantain	
buckeye	beardtongue, plantain, verbena, figwort	aster, chicory, coreopsis, false foxglove, milkweed
painted lady	mallow, thistle	aster, daisy, goldenrod, ironweed, yarrow
pearly crescentspot	aster	
red admiral (Vanessa)	nettle	ageratum, aster, thistle
silvery crescentspot	black-eyed susan, cone-flower, sunflower, aster	
variegated fritillary	passion flower, violet, stonecrop	
viceroy	willow, apple, cherry	
zebra longwing	passion flower	
Swallowtail		
eastern black	Queen Anne's lace	milkweed, phlox, Queen Anne's lace, thistle
tiger	ash, birch, cherry, sassafras, willow, cottonwood	ironweed, Joe Pye weed, phlox, sunflower
Gossamer Wings		
hairstreaks	mistletoe, red cedar, flame azalea, holly, blueberry	
Milkweed		
monarch	milkweed, butterfly weed	butterfly weed, milkweed, cosmos, goldenrod, Joe Pye weed, ironweed

Attracting Birds to Your Garden

Birds, in addition to being beautiful and having lovely songs, are useful as destroyers of harmful insects, beetles, and weed seeds. By ingesting the seed of numerous wildflowers, they are responsible for helping spread them from one area to another. The acid content of the bird's stomach acts as a natural scarifier of seed and aids in propagation.

Birds like to live in a natural wild landscape. Native trees, shrubs, and ground covers can be arranged to create habitats suitable for them. Offer them what they need — water, food, shelter and security. Mix trees, shrubs, vines and flowers in the right proportions to make your garden a more attractive and alluring bird habitat.

Water — for daily drinking, for bathing and preening. Use a shallow, rough bottomed bird bath. Change water frequently. Locate the bath in partial shade with safe refuge nearby.

Food — Plant a variety, give the birds a choice. You will need three kinds of plants:

1. Fruit bearers: blackberry, blueberry, crabapple, elderberry, mulberry, plum and wild cherry.

2. Insect attracters: maples, wild cherry and willows.

3. Seed producers: autumn olive (elaeagnus), bittersweet, coreopsis, dock, dogwood, goldenrod, heart's-a-bustin', holly, honeysuckle, magnolia, multiflora rose, phlox, polkweed, sumac, sunflower, thistle, and Virginia creeper.

Shelter — natural cover for shelter and security, for roosting, escape routes, windbreaks, and nesting sites. Different species of birds have special requirements. Plan and plant for a variety of naturalness and diversity including thickets. Cluster shrubs near watering spots: autumn olive (elaeagnus), barberry, dogwood, holly, honeysuckle, magnolia, and sassafras.

It is most important to keep a food and water supply steady, especially during dry or frozen periods. Provide some open areas planted with grasses for additional food. Hedges of autumn olive, holly, privet, serviceberry, etc., will attract bluebirds, cardinals, catbirds, chickadees, finches, grosbeaks, mockingbirds, orioles, robins, thrashers, thrushes and waxwings.

Ruby-Throated Hummingbird

This is the only hummingbird widely spread in the eastern United States and consequently in Georgia. They are attracted by bright red flowers, but will visit any color flowers in search of nectar and small insects. The flowers that attract the hummingbird, in addition to being red, are usually long and tubular, often drooping instead of upright. They contain abundant nectar. Good flowers for the hummingbird also provide for color in the wildflower garden all season. Spring — columbine and azalea. Summer — cardinal flower, bee balm, scarlet sage, touch-me-not. Fall — trumpet vine

Flowers That Produce Seed Suitable For Bird Food

aster	goldenrod	portulaca
bachelor buttons	ironweed	Solomon's seal
bee balm	jack-in-the-pulpit	spotted wintergreen
black-eyed susan	jewelweed	sunflower
blanket flower	Joe Pye weed	tickseed
butterfly weed	larkspur	violet
cardinal flower	lily of the valley	yarrow
columbine	lupine	VINES:
coneflower	milkweed	bittersweet
coreopsis	morning glory	blackberry
cosmos	ox-eye daisy	honeysuckle
day lily	partridge berry	trumpet vine
false Solomon's seal	phlox	Virginia creeper

IDENTIFYING WILD PLANTS

In identifying wild plants, or any plant for that matter, the first thing you have to do is see — really see. Look closely! It's important. You have to learn to look for more than the color of the flower. You have to learn to look for color on the leaf (bottom and top) and sometimes on the stem. You have to learn to look for the shape — shape of the petals, shape of the flower, shape of the head or inflorescence, shape of the stem, shape of the leaf, and shape of the leaflet. How is the leaf attached to the stem? What type edges does the leaf have? You must look for size — size of the stem, size of the flower, and size of the leaf. Is the flower and/or leaf smooth or hairy? Is it strong or delicate? Does the stem branch? Is it smooth or does it have thorns? Is the flower solitary or in a head? When does it bloom and for how long? When does it seed? What type of seed does it have? Is it deciduous or evergreen? The conditions under which the plant is found growing in the wild also help in identifying it. Where does it grow — deep woods, open woods, slopes, stream banks, roadsides, fields, etc? If in the woods, what type of woods is it? In what part of the state or country is it growing? Is the soil dry, moist or wet, acid or alkaline, loamy or sandy? Is it in the shade or in the sun or in between? What type of growth is it — herbaceous, woody, shrubby, vine, erect, prostrate? Does it have an odor? All of these conditions may help determine the plant's correct identification.

SYMBOLS:

LS: Lifespan   HT: Height   BL: Bloom Season

The number listed before each species description corresponds to the plate number listed with the photograph of that species (beginning on page 119). If there is no number, there is no photograph.

For easier identification photographs have been arranged in nine color groups — white, yellow, orange, pink (includes rose), red, purple (includes lavender and violet), blue, green and brown. Within the color groupings herbs, then ferns, shrubs, and trees, and vines have been arranged by family.

The caption accompanying the plate gives the plate identification number, one common name of the plant and the page number on which the species description is given.

WILDFLOWERS

Acanthus Family (*Acanthaceae*)

Perennial herbs or shrubs, leaves opposite, simple. Corolla usually irregular or two lipped, tubular, 4 - 5 sepals and 4 - 5 fused petals; calyx 4 - 5 parted. Seeds attached by hooked projections.

240 *Ruellia caroliniensis* Page 178
Hairy Ruellia, Wild Petunia
LS: Perennial HT: 1 - 2 1/2 ft. BL: May - July
Flower: Light purple or lavender blue, trumpet or funnel-shaped corolla with 5 flaring lobes and slender tube, open throat, grow in clusters of 2 to 4 in middle of upper leaf axils, stalkless or nearly so, about 1 - 1 1/2 in. across, open one at a time and remain open less than a day.
Leaves: Opposite, 2 - 2 1/2 in. long, oval to lanceolate, hairy, entire, two small leaves just below each pair of larger leaves, stem hairy.
Habitat: Open woods, clearings, sandy fields, rock crevices, banks.
Culture: Dry, moderately rich soil, light shade. Needs organic matter incorporated in soil.
Propagation: Seeds sown in the fall, cuttings, division.
Note: *Ruellia strepens* has stalked flowers and a smooth stem.

Amaryllis or Daffodil Family (*Amaryllidaceae*)

A family of herbaceous plants growing from bulbs or rhizomes. Flowers usually in umbels, lily-like with 6 petal-like parts, 6 stamens, often an inferior ovary, the whole inflorescence subtended by conspicuous bracts.

Hymenocallis caroliana
Spider lily
LS: Perennial HT: 1 - 1 1/2 ft. BL: April - June
Flower: White, 3 petals and 3 petal-like sepals, long and narrow, attached to slender tube with 6 radiating lobes. Lower half of stamens united at base to form a corolla-shaped crown, up to 7 in. across, 3 - 9 borne on a leafless stalk, fragrant.
Leaves: Basal, linear, 1/2 in. wide, 1 - 2 ft. long.
Habitat: Swamps, riverbanks, wooded slopes, marshes.
Culture: Damp rich soil.
Propagation: Seeds and offsets.

1 *Hymenocallis coronaria* Page 119
Spider lily
LS: Perennial HT: 15 - 20 in. BL: April - June
Flower: White, showy, up to 6 in. across, 3 petals and 3 petal-like sepals form perianth tube with 6 radiating lobes, lower half of stamens unite at the base to form a central cuplike crown and give a spidery appearance, 2 - 3 borne on a long, leafless scape, fragrant.

Leaves: Basal, linear or strap-shaped, up to 2 ft. long and 3/4 in. wide.
Habitat: Swamps, stream banks, shoals, marshes, bottomlands, wet spots.
Culture: Damp, rich soil.
Propagation: Seeds and offsets.
Note: Endangered species.

100 *Hypoxis hirsuta* Page 143
Star grass
LS: Perennial HT: 3 - 7 in. BL: May - July
Flower: Six bright yellow pointed petals form star-like, small, 1/2 in. wide flowers in clusters, hairy below.
Leaves: Basal, narrow and linear, stiff. Longer than flowering stems. Hairy.
Habitat: Meadows, open woods.
Culture: Sandy rich soil, neutral to acid, full to partial sun.
Propagation: Reseeds self. Collect and transplant small corms which grow from small bulb-like underground root that extends from the mother plant. Sow seeds in the fall.

2 *Zephyranthes atamsco* Page 119
Atamasco lily, Magic lily, Zephyr lily, Rain lily, Wild Easter lily
LS: Perennial HT: 6 - 15 in. BL: April - June
Flower: Large (3 1/2 in.), waxy, erect lily-like, white or pinkish, widest toward the tip, leafless flower stalk, usually single.
Leaves: Linear and flat.
Habitat: Moist woods, clearings, meadows.
Culture: Semi-shade or sun. Ordinary garden soil.
Propagation: By division of bulbs.

Arum Family (*Araceae*)

A large family of tropical herbs with fleshy or woody stems. Spathe usually surrounding spikelike spadix crowded with minute florets. Spathe absent in some species. Leaves usually long, smooth, and glossy, mostly basal.

300 *Arisaema dracontium* Page 193
Green dragon, Dragon root
LS: Perennial HT: 1 - 2 ft. BL: May - June
Flower: Long-tipped spadix (base covered with tiny greenish-yellow male and female flowers), extends several inches above narrow pointed and sheathing spathe. Fruit—cluster of orange-red berries.
Leaves: Single, compound (5 - 15 leaflets), dull green, oblong and pointed, 4 - 6 in. long.
Habitat: Rich, moist deciduous woods, stream banks.
Culture: Shade, moist humus-filled soil, neutral.
Propagation: Root division. Seed.

301 *Arisaema triphyllum* Page 194
Jack-in-the pulpit
LS: Perennial HT: 1 - 3 ft. BL: April
Flower: Predominately green, small flowers without petals closely packed on thick stem (spadix), hidden by hood-like spathe marked with white or purple stripes.

Leaves: Dull green, palmate, 3 lanceolate pointed leaflets compose one leaf. Each plant has 1 or 2 upright leaves on a long stem.
Habitat: Damp, deciduous woodland.
Culture: Acid, rich, humus-filled soil. Some shade.
Propagation: Clump of glossy red berries appears on spadix in the fall. When the seeds ripen, squeeze the pulp from around them and plant about 1/2 in. deep. Plants usually bloom 2 - 3 years after seed sown. Divide root offshoots in early spring or fall. Dig deep.

101 *Orontium aquaticum* Page 144
Golden club, Never wet
LS: Perennial HT: 8 - 12 in. BL: April - June
Flower: Minute, golden-yellow, closely packed on top portion of narrow cylindrical spadix for about 2 - 3 in., spathe a sheath around lower stalk (does not shelter spadix).
Leaves: Elliptical, dark green, basal, 6 - 12 in. long, parallel veined, may be floating or erect.
Habitat: Swamps, shallow streams, bogs.
Culture: Shade, shallow water.
Propagation: By seed or division of rootstock

Barberry Family (*Berberidaceae*)

A family of dissimilar genera made up of shrubs and perennial herbs. Flowers may have 6 - 9 waxy petals, 4 - 18 stamens. Leaves simple, deeply divided or compound with lobed leaflets, alternate or basal.

3 *Jeffersonia diphylla* Page 119
Twinleaf, Rheumatism root
LS: Perennial HT: 5 - 10 in. BL: April - May
Flower: White, 1 in. wide, solitary, 8 elongated petals, stalk leafless. Bloom short lived.
Leaves: Basal, long stemmed, 3 - 6 in. wide, deeply cleft into 2 kidney - shaped wings (almost completely divided). Leaf stem continues to grow taller after bloom fades.
Habitat: Open woods.
Culture: Rich, humus-filled, damp soil, neutral to slightly alkaline, partial shade. Mulch in fall.
Propagation: Seeds sown as soon as ripe. Divide in fall.
Note: Endangered.

4 *Podophyllum peltatum* Page 119
Mayapple
LS: Perennial HT: 12 - 18 in. BL: April - June
Flower: Single, large, waxy white, in stem crotch and below leaves. Ripe fruit—yellow apple.
Leaves: Two,large, peltate and deeply lobed, resembling an "umbrella".
Habitat: Rich deciduous, moist woods and meadows. Often grown in colonies.
Culture: Leaf mold soil, neutral to acid. Light shade.
Propagation: By seed, sown in the late fall as soon as they ripen. Self seeding. Spread rapidly. By root division. Bury rhizomes 1 - 2 in. deep with the tip pointing up. Easy to grow. Transplant without much difficulty. Best to transplant right after bloom fades.

Bedstraw or Madder Family (*Rubiaceae*)

Herbs, shrubs or trees with small corolla, funnel-shaped, usually 4 petals, 4 stamens, borne in a cyme or panicle. Leaves small and slender, opposite, whorled, simple.

293 *Hedyotis caerulea* (alternatively *Houstonia caerulea*) Page 192
Bluets, Quaker ladies
LS: Perennial HT: 2 - 6 in. BL: April - June
Flower: Dainty, petite, 1/2 in., 4 petals forming funnel-shaped corolla, solitary, blue or purple fading white, yellow eye. Blooms profusely.
Leaves: Basal rosette, others elliptical, opposite or whorled, on erect stem.

241 *Hedyotis crassifolia* (alternatively *Houstonia crassifolia*) Page 179
Bluets
LS: Annual HT: 2 - 6 in. BL: March - April
Flower: Violet to deep purple with dark pink or reddish eye, united petals.
Leaves: Opposite or whorled, stipuled, mostly near base of stem.

5 *Hedyotis purpurea* (alternatively *Houstonia purpurea*) Page 120
Bluets
LS: Perennial HT: 6 - 8 in. BL: April - June
Flower: Purple to lilac, pink or white, small, in clusters either terminal or in upper leaf axils.
Leaves: Oval, sessile, opposite, 3 - 5 ribs.
Note: *Hedyotis serpyllifolia* (Creeping bluets) have deep blue to purple flowers.
Habitat: (all species) Slopes, fields, meadows, full sun or light shade. Grow in colonies.
Culture: Moist, acid soil.
Propagation: By division before or after flowering. Spread by creeping rootstock. By seed. Also self seeding.

6 *Mitchella repens* Page 120
Partridge berry, Twinberry
LS: Perennial HT: 6 - 15 in. (Trailer) BL: June - July
Flower: Funnel-shaped, 4 fringed petals, white with pinkish tinge, 1/2 in. long, in pairs at ends of stems. Fruit—scarlet berry. Fragrant.
Leaves: Small, to 3/8 in., evergreen, opposite, rounded, dark green with white center stripe. Prostrate. Roots freely at joints, making flat patches.
Habitat: Dry or moist woods.
Culture: Shade or semi shade, good rich woods soil, acid.
Propagation: Division of rooted portions of stems. Seed.

Birthwort Family (*Aristolochiaceae*)

Herbs, shrubs or vines with large heart-shaped leaves, alternate, simple. Flowers have 3 triangular and flaring sepals (no petals), 6 - 36 stamens, inferior ovary.

315 *Asarum arifolium* (alternatively *Hexastylis arifolia*) Page 197

Heart leaf, Little brown jugs, Little pigs

LS: Perennial HT: 4 - 10 in. BL: April - May

Flower: Under the leaves and at ground level. Calyx flask or jug-shaped, less than 1 in. long, dull brown or purple. A flower without petals.

Leaves: Aromatic, thick, evergreen, triangular to ovate or heart-shaped with eared bases.

Habitat: Wooded slopes.

Culture: Moist to dry deciduous woods.

Propagation: By division.

316 *Asarum canadense* Page 197

Wild ginger, Canada ginger

LS: Perennial HT: 4 - 12 in. BL: April - May

Flower: Inconspicuous dull brownish purple and fuzzy. Calyx with a cup and 3 pointed lobes (jug-like). Grow under the leaves and at ground level at the base of the plant. A flower without petals.

Leaves: Cordate, deciduous, hairy.

Habitat: Rocky hillsides, deciduous woods.

Culture: Rich soil, full of leaf mold, slightly acid. Creeping habit makes a good ground cover.

Propagation: By root division. Transplant in early spring or fall. Creeping branching rootstock is slightly below the surface. Aromatic.

Bladderwort Family (*Lentibulariaceae*)

Aquatic or marsh herbs, insectivorous. Corolla 2 lipped, lower lip large, and 3 lobed with hollow spur, 2 stamens, borne on naked stalk, usually solitary. Leaves threadlike, underwater, equipped with bladder, or a rosette of fleshy basal leaves with curled edges.

242 *Pinguicula caerulea* Page 179

Violet butterwort

LS: Perennial HT: 2 - 6 in. BL: March - June

Flower: Small, solitary, violet, tubed corolla, 5 lobed, lower lobe spurred, borne on naked stem.

Leaves: Basal rosette, ovate, shiny and sticky, rolled in on edges, 2 in., yellow-green, carnivorous.

Habitat: Wet rocks, bogs, ditches, low pinelands.

Culture: Alkaline soil, sandy or peaty, moist.

Propagation: Seeds, offsets.

Bleeding Heart Family (*Fumariaceae*)

Annual and perennial herbs growing from corm-like rootstock. Flowers irregular (bilaterally symmetrical), 4 petals joined, 1 - 2 forming a swollen spur, borne in racemes. Leaves finely cut and dissected.

7 *Dicentra cucullaria* Page 120
Dutchman's breeches
LS: Perennial HT: 10 - 12 in. BL: April - May
Flower: Small and nodding, white or cream, in raceme on slender stalk about the leaves. Two diverging pantaloon shaped spurs on corolla form "dutchman's breeches." Not fragrant.
Leaves: Deciduous, thrice compound, feathery and much divided, gray-green, paler on underside.

8 *Dicentra canadensis* Page 120
Squirrel corn
LS: Perennial HT: 6 - 12 in. BL: April
Flower: Small, white to pale pink, heart-shaped with short, rounded spurs, in drooping, terminal clusters. Corolla base cordate.
Leaves: Blue green, feathery, deciduous.

175 *Dicentra eximia* Page 162
Fringed bleeding heart
LS: Perennial HT: 9 - 18 in. BL: April - May
Flower: Small, pink to deep rose, rounded heart-shaped flowers with a "drop of blood" between 2 flaring wings, borne in panicles.
Leaves: Graceful, fernlike.
Habitat: (all species) Rich, deciduous open woods, ledges.
Culture: Partial shade with filtered sunlight, moist soil, good drainage, slightly acid to neutral soil (bleeding heart prefers more acid soil). All 3 naturalize easily.
Propagation: Divide plants when crowded. Gather seeds from capsules as soon as they ripen. Barely cover seeds with soil. Takes several years to bloom.

Corydalis flavula
Yellow fumewort, Yellow corydalis, Yellow harlequin
LS: Perennial HT: 6 - 16 in. BL: April - May
Flower: Pale yellow, 2 small sepals, 4 petals (2 pairs—upper pair with a toothed crest and with a long hollow spur that projects backwards, 2 inner petals join at tip and have a projecting wing), 6 stamen, about 1/2 in. long, borne in loose dangling clusters.
Leaves: Finely cut, delicate with whitish bloom.
Habitat: Open woods, rocks.
Culture: Sandy or gravel soil, porous, sun or partial shade.
Propagation: Seeds, division.
Note: *Corydalis aurea* (golden corydalis) has golden yellow flowers with short, stubby petals without a crest and is native north of the southeast. *Corydalis micrantha* (slender fumewort) has a smooth-marginal crest with flowers smaller and more compact and is found on sandy soils of South Georgia.

Bluebell or Bellflower Family (*Campanulaceae*)

Usually herbs (annual, biennial and perennial) made up of 2 sub-families.

1. Bluebell sub-family: Corolla usually bell-shaped with 5 flaring lobes, 5 stamens, single style, 2-5 lobed stigma. Leaves undivided and alternate.
2. Lobellia sub-family (*Lobelioideae*): Corolla tube opens along upper side, 2 lobes on upper lip and 3 lobes on drooping lower lip, stamens joined together in a tube. Leaves alternate. Exudes a milky juice.

243 *Campanula divaricata* Page 179
Southern harebell, Bellflower
LS: Perennial HT: 6 - 24 in. BL: July - September
Flower: Corolla pale blue or purple, bell shaped, 1/3 in. long or less, numerous, dangle from horizontal branchlets.
Leaves: Lanceolate to ovate, small.
Habitat: Roadsides, rocky woods, grassy meadows.
Culture: Dry to damp soil, partial to full sun.
Propagation: Seed, division.

217 *Lobelia cardinalis* Page 173
Cardinal flower
LS: Perennial HT: 2 - 4 ft. BL: July - September
Flower: Brilliant red with 5 petals, form a 2 lipped tubular corolla. Grow in an elongated cluster or spike on an erect stalk.
Leaves: Long, alternate, lanceolate, slightly toothed. Deep green leafy rosette at bottom.
Habitat: Stream banks, swamps, damp areas.
Culture: Damp spots, sun or half shade. Root system shallow and fibrous. Temperamental.
Propagation: Sow seeds in spring. Keep moist. May take cuttings in midsummer. Root divide in spring or fall.

244 *Lobelia inflata* Page 179
Indian tobacco
LS: Annual HT: 6 - 18 in. BL: July - October
Flower: Lavender, pale blue, violet, 1/4 in., tucked in leaf axils in a loose spike.
Leaves: Ovate, toothed, 1 - 2 1/2 in. long, thin, light green.
Habitat: Fields, roadsides, open woods.
Culture: Dry, average garden soil. Poison.
Propagation: Seed.

245 *Lobelia puberula* Page 180
Downy lobelia
LS: Perennial HT: 1 - 3 ft. BL: July - October
Flower: Five petals form a two-lipped tubular corolla, light blue or purple with a white eye, 1/2 - 3/4 in. long, usually borne on one side of the stem.
Leaves: Ovate to lanceolate, hairy on lower side, stem hairy.
Habitat: Roadsides, open woods, clearings.
Culture: Wet soil, partial to full sun.
Propagation: Seed, division.

294 *Lobelia siphilitica* Page 192

Great lobelia

LS: Perennial HT: 2 - 3 ft. BL: August - September

Flower: Deep, bright blue (sometimes pink or white), to 1 in. long, 2 lipped, striped white on lip of lower lobe. Borne singly in leaf axils in an elongated spike.

Leaves: Alternate, oval, pointed at both ends, 2 - 6 in. long.

Habitat: Along streams, damp woods, meadows, swamps.

Culture: Moist or wet soil, slightly acidic, fairly rich, semi shade.

Propagation: Seed sown late in fall. Stem cuttings.

Note: The combination of blue great lobelia with red cardinal flower makes an awesome perennial garden border.

246 *Specularia perfoliata* (alternatively *Triodanis perfoliata*) Page 180

Venus looking glass

LS: Annual HT: 6 - 15 in. BL: May - August

Flower: Dainty, violet-blue, 1/2 - 3/4 in. across, 5 lobed. Borne in leaf axils, usually singly. Stemless. Flowers grow along an erect slender stem that is angled and hairy. Lower flowers on stem do not open (produce seed).

Leaves: Round (shell-shaped), scalloped, clasping, alternate.

Habitat: Open fields, dry woods, roadsides.

Culture: Dry, often poor soil.

Propagation: Fruit many seeded. Sow in spring or fall.

Specularia biflora is similar but leaves do not clasp the stem.

Note: Tiny flowers are good for pressing.

Broomrape Family (*Orobanchaceae*)

Fleshy, root parasites with 5-lobed corolla (united petals) with upper and lower lip. Leaves alternate and scalelike.

102 *Conopholis americana* Page 144

Squaw root

LS: Perennial HT: 3 - 9 in. BL: May - July

Flower: Yellow, 1/3 in. long, irregular, in upper scale axils, bloom 4 - 6 in. long.

Leaves: Ovate, scale-like, crowded all over the stem (looks like slender pine cone), yellow-tan. Usually several "cones" in a tight cluster.

Habitat: Woods, under oak or beech trees.

Culture: Parasite on roots of oak or beech trees.

9 *Orobanche uniflora* Page 121

One-flowered cancer-root

LS: Perennial HT: 3 - 8 in. BL: April - June

Flower: Five nearly equal lobes, tubular, 3/4 - 1 in. long, creamy white to pale purple or lavender, borne singly on stem tip.

Leaves: Minute scales near base of naked, sticky stalk.

Habitat: Woods.

Culture: Rich soil, moist, shade.

Propagation: Parasite.

Buttercup or Crowfoot Family (*Ranunculaceae*)

Mostly perennial herbs, occasionally woody climbers, growing from rhizomes or condensed rootstock. Following years' growth develops from basal axillary bud. Flowers solitary, in racemes or panicles, 6 - 10 showy sepals replace petals in many species, numerous stamens and pistils.

10, *Actaea pachypoda* (formerly *Actaea alba*) Page 121
11 Baneberry, Doll's eyes
LS: Perennial HT: 1 - 2 ft. BL: April - June
Flower: Small, white, very narrow petals, numerous, in oblong terminal racemes, feathery appearance. Berries: Showy, borne singly on short reddish stem, oval, spotted purple-black at the ends.
Leaves: Compound, leaflets cleft and toothed, lobes sharply pointed. Stems branching.
Habitat: Woods, thickets.
Culture: Rich woodsy soil, partial shade, moisture, slightly acidic to neutral.
Propagation: From seed (remove pulp). Bloom 3rd year. By division in fall or spring. Fruits appear July - September.
Note: Poisonous

218 *Aquilegia canadensis* Page 173
Columbine
LS: Perennial HT: 1 - 3 ft. BL: April - June
Flower: Pendant red and yellow bell-like flowers with 5 long spurs or petals pointing upward and numerous yellow stamen hanging down.
Leaves: Fine, compound, long stalked. Divided into 3-lobed leaflets. Bluish green. Stems branching and slender.
Habitat: Dry banks, slopes, rocky ledges, woodland clearings.
Culture: Slightly acid soil, moist and well drained. Soil should not be too rich. Light shade.
Propagation: By seed sown as soon as ripe, usually July. Self seeding. Bloom second year after planting. May move young plants in late fall or early spring but they have a deep seated rootstock. Set roots at crown level. Established plants are hard to move.
Note: Attracts hummingbirds.

Anemone quinquefolia
Wood anemone, Windflower
LS: Perennial HT: 4 - 8 in. BL: April - May
Flower: White, petal-like sepals tinged pink, usually 5, solitary, delicate.
Leaves: Basal, compound, whorled with 5 leaflets or 3 leaflets with laterals, sharply toothed.
Habitat: Open woodlands, clearings.
Culture: Moist, woodsy, slightly acidic soil, light shade.
Propagation: Root cuttings. Divide root segments in spring. By seed sown as soon as ripe. Flower in 2 - 3 years.

12 *Anemone virginiana* Page 121
Thimbleweed, Tall anemone
LS: Perennial HT: 2 - 3 ft. BL: July - August

Flower: 4 - 9 greenish to white, small sepals, borne on long upright flower stalks, solitary.
Fruit: Oblong thimble-like seed head.
Leaves: Palmately cleft, opposite, wedge-shaped.
Habitat: Woods, meadows, roadsides.
Culture: Light shade, rich well-drained slightly acidic soil.
Propagation: Seeds. Division while dormant.

13 *Anemonella thalictroides* (alternatively *Thalictrum thalictroides*) Page 122
Rue anemone
LS: Perennial HT: 6 - 8 in. BL: April - May
Flower: Delicate, 1/2 - 1 in. wide, white petal-like sepals (6 - 10), 2 or 3 to a forked stem.
Leaves: Basal, compound, oval, 3 round-lobed leaflets, whorled just below bloom. Slender, weak stems.
Habitat: Wooded slopes, deciduous open woods.
Culture: Moist soil, acidic, light shade, protection from wind.
Propagation: Division of tubers after foliage dies down. Sow seed after they ripen. Flower 2nd year. Also self seeding.

14 *Hepatica acutiloba* Page 122
Sharp-lobed hepatica, Liverleaf
LS: Perennial HT: 6 - 8 in. BL: March - May
Flower: Lilac, pale purple to white, 1/2 - 1 in. wide, 5 - 10 petal like sepals, appear before leaves.
Leaves: Basal, 3-lobed, oval, sharply pointed, mottled. Die after flowers fade; new ones appear and stay evergreen.

176 *Hepatica americana* Page 162
Round-lobed hepatica, Liverleaf
LS: Perennial HT: 6 - 9 in. BL: March - May
Flower: Blue, white or pink, 5 - 10 petal-like sepals, 1/2 - 1 in. wide, appear before the leaves, 3 bracts below the flower.
Leaves: Basal, heart-shaped, rounded, 3-lobed. Die after flowers fade; new ones appear and stay evergreen.
Habitat: (both species) Rocky hillsides, open woods.
Culture: Neutral to slightly acidic soil, humus rich, semi-shade.
Propagation: Divide root clumps (rhizomes) in fall. Sow seed as soon as they ripen (catch in a tied-on plastic bag). Tend to colonize.
Note: *H. americana* is sometimes referred to as *H. triloba*, sometimes placed as varieties under European *H. nobilis*.

15 *Hydrastis canadensis* Page 122
Golden seal
LS: Perennial HT: 5 - 9 in. BL: April - May
Flower: Solitary and inconspicuous. No petals or sepals. Many white stamens. Wiry appearance.
Leaves: One leaf and/or one stem with 2 leaves near top, very wrinkled. Leaves enlarge after flowering.
Habitat: Coniferous or deciduous woodland.
Culture: Partial to full shade. Moist humus-rich soil, slightly acidic.

Propagation: Seed hard to germinate.
Note: Very rare—endangered species. Do not pick. Be extremely careful if transplanting.

103 *Ranunculus bulbosus* Page 144
Bulbous buttercup
LS: Perennial HT: 6 - 18 in. BL: April - June
Flower: Glossy, small, 1 in. wide, deep bright yellow, reflexed sepals (3 - 5, downward pointing, green), 5 petals, many busy yellow stamens. Borne in loose corymb.
Leaves: Basal, deeply cut, palmate (3 segments, *end one* stalked), 1 - 4 in. wide, upright with long petioles. Stem leaves smaller, palmate, 5 - 7 narrow leaflets, toothed, sessile, alternate.
Habitat: Fields, roadsides, meadows.
Culture: Ordinary soil, sun or partial shade.
Propagation: Seed. Division of bulbous roots every 3 years.
Note: An escape, native of Europe and North Africa. Tends to be weedy. Identificaiton difficult. *R. acris* (common buttercup, tall buttercup) grows 2 - 3 ft. was naturalized from Eurasia, often cultivated with double flowers.

104 *Ranunculus repens* Page 144
Creeping buttercup
LS: Perennial HT: 4 - 8 in. BL: May - June
Flower: Deep yellow, single, often mottled, sepals hairy, 5 petals, many stamens.
Leaves: Deep green, oval, wavy margins. Deciduous. Runners root at joints.
Habitat: Open fields, low lands, woodland edges.
Culture: Wet or moist ground, semi-shade.
Propagation: By seed or division.
Note: An escape, naturalized from Eurasia, Tends to be aggressive.

Thalictrum dioicum
Early meadow-rue
LS: Perennial HT: 8 - 30 in. BL: April - May
Flower: Drooping, greenish-white, small (1/4 in.), without petals, 4 - 5 sepals, borne in terminal and axillary clusters. Male and female flowers on separate plants. Male flowers have showy yellow stamens, female flowers have purplish pistils.
Leaves: Leaflets short, upper leaves petioled, leaflets 3 - 4 lobed, pale underneath.
Habitat: Rich dry to moist woods.
Culture: Light rich, loamy soil, well drained.
Propagation: Seed, division in very early spring.

16 *Thalictrum polygamum* Page 122
Tall meadow-rue
LS: Perennial HT: 4 - 8 ft. BL: May - August
Flower: Greenish-white, very small, about 1/3 in., petals lacking, threadlike stamens numerous, borne in large, loosely branched terminal clusters, feathery appearance. Pistillate and staminate flowers.
Leaves: Compound, leaflets oval, 3 lobed, small (similar to Maidenhair Fern), alternate, light olive green above, paler below. Branching habit.
Habitat: Damp woods, meadows, roadsides.

Culture: Light, rich loamy soil, slightly acid, light shade.
Propagation: Seeds—require two years to bloom. Division.
Note: Attracts butterflies.

Cactus Family (*Cactaceae*)

Perennial, mostly succulent, trees, shrubs or shrublets with large cuplike flowers with many petals, numerous stamens and stigmas. Leafless, spiny modified fleshy stems.

105 *Opuntia compressa* Page 145
Prickly pear
LS: Perennial HT: 6 - 10 in. BL: July - August
Flower: Bright yellow, large, up to 3 in. wide, 10 - 12 petals, numerous stamens, reddish toward center. Fruit shaped like a small pear.
Leaves: Inconspicuous. Fall early. Deep green, flat, fleshy and very prickly oval stem segments known as joints. Prostrate habit.
Habitat: Sandy areas, open rocky sites.
Culture: Sandy soil, dry conditions.
Propagation: Separate joints (be very careful of barbs) and root in dry sand.

Cattail Family (*Typhaceae*)

Small family of aquatic herbs, leaves long, erect stem, head cylindrical, made up of tightly packed brown and minute pistillate flowers, topped by staminate flowers; 2 - 5 stamens. Creeping rootstock.

317 *Typha angustifolia* Page 198
Cat-tail, Narrow leafed
LS: Perennial HT: 2 - 6 ft. BL: June - July
Flower: Not as dark in color or as thick as *T. latifolia* (see next) and more delicate. Gap separates male and female flowers.
Leaves: Very narrow (to 1/2 in. wide).
Habitat, Culture, Propagation: See next.

318 *Typha latifolia* Page 198
Cat-tail, Broad leafed
LS: Perennial HT: 2 - 8 ft. BL: June - July
Flower: Staminate (male) yellowish flower spikes uppermost on stalk (drop after pollen sheds). Pistillate (female) dark brown spikes lower (slightly separated but on same plant), hundreds densely packed on cylindrical terminal spikes, 3 - 10 in. long, 1 in. thick.
Leaves: Linear, flat (sword like), erect, sheathed at base. Green. Taller than flowering stem.
Habitat: (both species) Bogs, swamps, wet ground, shallow ponds.
Culture: Sun or semi-shade, shallow water.

Propagation: By division or by seeds planted in pots kept in water. Rampant growers—usually in thick colonies (plant in shallow water in containers to keep from spreading).
Note: Dry by picking before seed pods ripen. Spray with hair spray to preserve.

Composite, Daisy or Sunflower Family (*Compositae*)

Mostly herbs. Flowers usually flat shaped, ray florets arranged around many small disc florets in the center, borne above bracts (some lack ray florets), usually borne in clusters though may be solitary. Leaves alternate (rarely opposite or whorled), simple or dissected.

17, 177 *Achillea millefolium* — Pages 123, 163
Yarrow
LS: Perennial   HT: 1 - 2 ft.   BL: June - September
Flower: Very small, white, sometimes pink. Disk flowers surrounded by 4 - 6 ray flowers. Numerous, forming flat topped tight clusters.
Leaves: Finely cut, fernlike, gray-green, strongly aromatic; stem hairy.
Habitat: Open fields, roadsides.
Culture: Full sun. Ordinary garden soil.
Propagation: By division of rootstock—creeping underground stem.
Note: Naturalized from Eurasia. Aggressive growth habit.

18 *Antennaria solitaria* — Page 123
Field pussytoes, Solitary pussytoes
LS: Perennial   HT: 6 - 12 in.   BL: May - July
Flower: All disk flowers enclosed by greenish bracts with white tips, borne in a single head, on an erect woolly stem, fuzzy white, up to 1/2 in. in diameter.
Leaves: Spoon-shaped, basal, arranged in a rosette, woolly, dull green above, silvery white below, 3 - 5 main veins. Leaves on stem small and lanceolate.
Habitat: Lawns, pastures, thin open woods, rocky meadows.
Culture: Dry soils.
Propagation: Plants spread by creeping runners or stolons putting down new roots at their tips. Separate and divide.
Note: Tends to colonize. Flower cluster resembles a cat's paw. Male and female blooms borne on different plants. Female plants are taller. Male blooms are smaller and more highly colored. *Antennaria plantaginifolia* (Plantain-leaved Pussytoes) is similar to *A. solitaria* but not as woolly.

247 *Aster novae-angliae* — Page 180
New England purple aster
LS: Perennial   HT: 2 - 5 ft.   BL: July - October
Flower: Purple, violet, pink or white ray florets, prominent yellow disk florets, forming daisy-like bloom, 1 - 2 in. in diameter, clustered at end of branches in large panicles.
Leaves: Long, narrow, stem-clasping, 3 - 4 in. long, numerous. Short, copiously hairy, somewhat sticky stems.
Habitat: Fields, along streams, meadows, woodland openings.
Culture: Well-drained garden soil, full sun to light shade, moist. Pinching encourages branching.

Propagation: By seed, sown in the fall. Germination poor. Divide clumps in fall or spring every 2 - 3 years. Transplant in spring.
Note: Sometimes naturalized in the southeast, not native to Georgia area.

Berlandiera pumila
Green eyes
LS: Perennial HT: 2 - 3 ft. BL: May - September
Flower: Yellow ray florets, green disk florets, becoming red-maroon with age, 1 - 2 in. across. Bracts just below the bloom. Broad, sunflower like.
Leaves: Alternate, hairy, coarsely crenate, borne on woolly gray stems. Most leaves are basal.
Habitat: Thin woods, open fields, pinelands.
Culture: Sandy soil.
Propagation: Seed.

106 *Bidens aristosa* Page 145
Tickseed sunflower, Stick tight
LS: Annual HT: 1 - 4 ft. BL: August - October
Flower: Daisy-like, showy yellow ray florets 1 in. long, darker yellow disk florets, up to 10 ray florets per bloom, 2 in. wide. Bracts beneath head of two distinct types, as in coreopsis.
Leaves: Linear, deeply and regularly toothed, opposite, 2 - 6 in. long.
Habitat: Roadsides, fields, hollows.
Culture: Full to partial sun, prefer moist soil but will grow under dry conditions.
Propagation: Seeds sown in fall. Self seeding. Transplant seedlings in spring.
Note: Many other species found in area; often extremely showy when planted in mass.

248 *Centaurea cyanus* Page 180
Cornflower, Bachelor's buttons
LS: Annual HT: 1 - 2 ft. BL: April - July
Flower: Head 1 1/2 in. across, deep blue (may also be white, rose, purple or mauve), single or double, tubular florets only (marginal florets ray like). Numerous overlapping toothed bracts below heads.
Leaves: Narrow, long, linear, untoothed, woolly when young, green when older. Stem branched.
Habitat: Fields, roadsides.
Culture: Good garden soil, sun.
Propagation: Seed. Often reseeds self.
Note: An escape from Europe and Near East.

19 *Chrysanthemum leucanthemum* (alternatively *Leucanthemum vulgare*) Page 123
Ox-eye daisy
LS: Perennial HT: 1 - 2 ft. BL: June - September
Flower: Head daisy-like, 2 in. wide, ray florets white, disc florets bright yellow and depressed, solitary.
Leaves: Narrow, sessile, irregularly lobed, dark green, alternate.
Habitat: Meadows, fields, roadsides.
Culture: Ordinary soil.

Propagation: Seeds. Roots tenacious. Hard to divide.
Note: An escape from Eurasia; widely naturalized. Tends to be aggressive.

107 *Chrysogonum virginianum* Page 145
Green and gold, Golden star
LS: Perennial HT: 4 - 7 in. BL: March - October
Flower: Five yellow ray florets surround flat yellow disk florets, up to 1 in. wide, daisy like. Green bracts alternate with yellow rays, hence the name green and gold.
Leaves: Dark green, heart-shaped, long stalked, opposite, hairy.
Habitat: Open woods.
Culture: Partial sun, rich woodsy, well-drained soil.
Propagation: Divide and transplant trailers.
Note: The southern variety *C. australe* naturally produces runners. The northern variety *C. virginianum* is taller and less suitable as a ground cover.

108 *Chrysopsis mariana* Page 145
Maryland golden aster
LS: Perennial HT: 1 - 3 ft. BL: July - September
Flower: Yellow ray and disc florets, flower up to 1 in. wide, forming loose small terminal corymbs. Bracts below flowers sticky.
Leaves: Basal rosette, cauline leaves alternate, oblong, woolly or hairy, lanceolate, 1 - 2 in. long.
Habitat: Fields, roadsides, meadows.
Culture: Dry, sandy soil, sun to light shade.
Propagation: Seed. Division in spring. Transplants easily.

295 *Cichorium intybus* Page 192
Chicory, Blue sailors, Succory
LS: Perennial HT: 1 - 3 ft. BL: June - October
Flower: Clear sky blue (rarely white or pink), stalkless, ray florets only (12 - 20 per flower), square tipped and fringed, terminal or in leaf axils of upper leaves, in heads to 1 1/2 in. in diameter. Each bloom lasts only 1 day and closes by noon.
Leaves: Basal, oblong and numerous, stem leaves very small and clasping, alternate, contain milky juice.
Habitat: Roadsides, fields.
Culture: Ordinary soil.
Propagation: Divide young roots and plant in spring. Seed.
Note: An escape from Mediterranean area. Seeds attract goldfinches; leaves used as salad greens; parsnip-like roots dried and ground as a coffee substitute.

109 *Coreopsis lanceolata* Page 146
Lanceleaf coreopsis
LS: Perennial HT: 1 - 3 ft. BL: May - September
Flower: Daisy-like, solitary, 2 in. wide, 8 yellow rays (petals) with 4 deep lobes on top, numerous disk florets (center); bracts beneath heads of two types—outer leafy, inner scale-like, both types joined at base.
Leaves: Basal and lower lance-shaped sometimes with lateral lobes; upper opposite, linear, unstalked.

110 *Coreopsis major* Page 146

Tall coreopsis, Tickseed

LS: Perennial HT: 2 - 3 ft. BL: May - September

Flower: 8 yellow rays (petals), notched, surrounding many yellow disk flowers, daisy like, 2 - 2 1/2 in.

Leaves: Wide, opposite (appear whorled), each leaf divided into 3 segments.

Habitat: (both species) Thin woods, dry places, grassy fields.

Culture: Ordinary, dry, well drained sandy or rocky soil, full sun.

Propagation: From seed sown in fall or spring. Division of clumps.

178 *Cosmos bipinnatus* Page 163

Cosmos

LS: Annual HT: 2 - 4 ft. BL: July - October

Flower: Showy pink, white or lilac, single, in heads 1 - 3 in. wide, 8 scalloped or notched ray florets surrounding yellow disc florets.

Leaves: Narrow, finely cut into many segments giving feathery appearance, opposite, weak erect stems.

Habitat: Roadsides, fields, railroad banks.

Culture: Average soil (preferably sandy), sun or partial shade. Pinch to encourage bushiness.

Propagation: Seed sown in the spring.

Note: An escape from Mexico.

249 *Eupatorium coelestinum* (alternatively *Conoclinium coelestinum*) Page 181

Mistflower, Wild ageratum, Blue boneset

LS: Perennial HT: 1 - 2 ft. BL: August - October

Flower: Tiny, tubular only, lavender or blue violet, crowded in 3 - 4 in. flat topped heads or clusters, fuzzy appearance (ageratum-like), borne on branching stems.

Leaves: Opposite, triangular, coarsely toothed. Deciduous.

Habitat: Thickets, roadsides, open woods, along streams.

Culture: Well-drained soil, sun or light shade, moisture. Cut back to encourage branching.

Propagation: Divide clumps (may be matted). Sow seed in spring or fall. Self seeding. May spread rapidly.

179 *Echinacea laevigata* Page 163

Purple coneflower

LS: Perennial HT: 18 - 36 in. BL: May - July

Flower: Deep to pale pink ray flowers, drooping.

Leaves: Similar to *E. purpurea* (see next) but usually smooth to touch; stems rarely branched, smooth.

Habitat: Meadows and woodlands.

Culture: Basic soil.

Propagation: Seed or division.

Note: Threatened species in Georgia.

250 *Echinacea purpurea* Page 181
Purple coneflower
LS: Perennial HT: 2 - 4 ft. BL: June - October
Flower: Showy, 3 - 5 in., daisylike and solitary, magenta or purple ray florets. Dark orange-brown center disk florets, prickly and conical in shape. Long lasting. Ray florets angle downward at maturity.
Leaves: Basal, coarse and sharply toothed. Other leaves alternate, ovate, rough, toothed. Stout hairy stems sometimes branched.
Habitat: Fields, roadsides, open woods.
Culture: Full to partial sun. Rich moist or dry soil. Easy to grow.
Propagation: By seed or division. Transplant easily when moved with large ball of soil.

251 *Elephantopus tomentosus* Page 181
Elephant foot
LS: Perennial HT: 10 - 15 in. BL: August - September
Flower: Pink to purple, tubular florets only, 1/2 in. wide, surrounded by 3 bracts. Borne in heads on almost bare stems that branch near the top.
Leaves: Basal rosette, broad, hairy underneath, hug the ground, oblong. Deciduous.
Habitat: Open woods, dry fields, roadsides.
Culture: Acid soil, sun or semi-shade.
Propagation: Seed. Self seeding. Tends to be aggressive.

20 *Erigeron strigosus* Page 123
Daisy fleabane
LS: Perennial HT: 2 - 4 ft. BL: May - August
Flower: Small, 1/2 in. wide, daisy like, numerous white ray florets, yellow disc florets. Borne in clusters.
Leaves: Narrow near top, ovate lower on branched, hairy stem. Strongly toothed.
Habitat: Fields, roadsides, wood edges.
Culture: Acid soil, sun or semi-shade.
Propagation: Seed. Self seeding.

21 *Eupatorium rugosum* Page 124
Snakeroot, White snakeroot
LS: Perennial HT: 1 - 3 ft. BL: July - October
Flower: White, very small, fuzzy, all disk florets borne in flat-topped clusters on branching stems.
Leaves: Opposite, long petioled, heart shaped or deltoid, coarsely toothed.
Habitat: Rich woods, fields.
Culture: Shade, rich humus filled soil.
Propagation: Seed. Division.
Note: Plants poisonous to livestock, causing milk sickness in humans.

252 *Eupatorium fistuloum* Page 181
Hollow Joe Pye weed, Queen of the meadow
LS: Perennial HT: 7 - 10 ft. BL: July - September
Flower: Light mauve to light purple. Dense fuzzy clusters make up large, rounded terminal inflorescence, composed entirely of tubular blossoms.

Leaves: Usually lanceolate, coarsely toothed. Arranged in whorls of 4 - 7. Stems stout, hollow, smooth, purplish throughout.

Eupatorium maculatum
Spotted Joe Pye weed
LS: Perennial HT: 2 - 7 ft. BL: July - September
Flower: Deeper in color than *E. fistuloum* and *E. purpureum*. Inflorescence more flat topped.
Leaves: Narrow and lanceolate, usually 3 - 5, whorled, coarsely toothed. Stems purple or purple spotted, not hollow.

253 *Eupatorium purpureum* Page 182
Sweet Joe Pye weed
LS: Perennial HT: 4 - 9 ft. BL: July - September
Flower: Corolla pale pink or purplish, fuzzy, numerous flowers grouped into large rounded or pyramidal head.
Leaves: Oval or ovate-lanceolate, whorls of 3 - 4 along the stem, coarsely toothed. Stem green, purple at leaf joints, stout, not hollow. Vanilla odor when crushed.
Habitat: (all species) Meadows, along streams and woodsides.
Culture: Moist soil, light shade or sun.
Propagation: Division of clumps in the spring. Sow seed in spring or fall. Self seeding. Easy to cultivate.

219 *Gaillardia pulchella* Page 173
Fire wheel, Indian blanket
LS: Annual HT: 8 - 16 in. BL: June - September
Flower: Daisy-like, 1 - 3 in. wide, ray florets red or maroon with yellow tip. Disk florets same color as rays. Bracts overlap. Solitary, borne on erect stems.
Leaves: Alternate, lower pinnate, upper lanceolate, 1 - 3 in. long, hairy.
Habitat: Fields, roadsides where naturalized; native along the seacoast.
Culture: Sandy soil, well drained, full sun.
Propagation: Seed sown in the spring.

22 *Gnaphalium obtusifolium* Page 124
Sweet everlasting, Rabbit tobacco
LS: Biennial HT: 1 - 3 ft. BL: August - October
Flower: Disk florets, 1/4 in., whitish-yellow, overlapped by bracts, arranged in many flowered heads. Fragrant (tobacco-like). No ray florets.
Leaves: First year - rosette, oblong. Second year - alternate, sessile, light green, hairy below, lanceolate, 1 - 4 in.
Habitat: Fields, pastures, roadsides, thin woods.
Culture: Sandy soil.
Propagation: Seed. Division of clumps.
Note: Good for drying. *Anaphalis margaritacea* (pearly everlasting) is commonly seen further north than Georgia. Its florets are embedded in conspicuous dry, pearly white bracts.

111 *Helianthus atrorubens* Page 146
Hairy sunflower
LS: Perennial HT: 5 - 9 ft. BL: June - October
Flower: Golden yellow rays, dark purple to brown center, 3 in. across.
Leaves: Mostly basal, long elegant stem with 1 - 2 smaller pairs of ovate leaves.

112 *Helianthus angustifolius* Page 146
Narrow-leaved sunflower
LS: Perennial HT: 1 - 4 ft. BL: June - October
Flower: Bright yellow rays, reddish purple disk, 2 - 3 in. across.
Leaves: Deep green, glossy, very narrow, lanceolate, branched stem.

113 *Helianthus divaricatus* Page 147
Woodland sunflower
LS: Perennial HT: 2 - 7 ft. BL: July - September
Flower: Yellow ray and disk flowers, 2 - 2 1/2 in. across, bracts lanceolate, outer ones spreading.
Leaves: Lanceolate, round at base, tapering to a long point, toothed, 3 - 8 in. long, rough above, hairy below, sessile or on short stalks, usually opposite.

114 *Helianthus hirsutus* Page 147
Stiff sunflower, Rough sunflower
LS: Perennial HT: 2 - 6 ft. BL: August - September
Flower: Yellow ray and disk flowers, 2 - 3 in. across.
Leaves: Opposite, petioled, ovate to lanceolate, stems hairy or rough.

Helianthus longifolius
Narrow-leaved sunflower
LS: Perennial HT: 3 - 5 ft. BL: July - September
Flower: Yellow ray and disk florets, 2 in. wide.
Leaves: Very narrow, 3 - 4 in. long, opposite, short stalked.

Helianthus resinosus (erroneously called *Helianthus tomentosus*)
Woolly sunflower
LS: Perennial HT: 3 - 6 ft. BL: June - October
Flower: Yellow rays, yellow centers, 2 - 4 in. across; bracts beneath head strongly reflexed.
Leaves: Hairy, velvety beneath; lanceolate to ovate, mostly alternate.

115 *Helianthus tuberosus* Page 147
Jerusalem artichoke
LS: Perennial HT: 5 - 9 ft. BL: June - October
Flower: Yellow ray, yellow disk, to 3 in. wide, several borne in terminal cluster.
Leaves: Broad, thick, rough, lanceolate. Hairy stems rough and branching, opposite leaves lower stem, alternate upper stem. Grayish.
Habitat: (all species) Fields, roadsides.
Culture: Moist soil, some sand, acid to neutral soil, full sun. Pinch to encourage bushier, shorter growth.

Propagation: Seed, Division of root clumps.
Note: Most species difficult to identify.

Liatris elegans
Pale blazing star
LS: Perennial HT: 2 - 4 ft. BL: August - October
Flower: White to pinkish disk florets; heads relatively small with 5 florets, bracts very hairy, pointed, nearly spine-tipped.
Leaves: Numerous, narrow, upper ones soon deciduous and often pointed downward.
Note: Most unusual Liatris for Georgia.

254 *Liatris scariosa* Page 182
Large blazing star
LS: Perennial HT: 2 - 4 ft. BL: July - September
Flower: Rose purple, disk florets along upper part of stem in uninterrupted spike; heads relatively large with more than 15 florets; bracts rounded, purplish, often dry, thin margins.
Leaves: Alternate, narrow, lanceolate, numerous, deciduous.

255 *Liatris spicata* Page 182
Dense blazing star, Gay feather
LS: Perennial HT: 2 - 4 ft. BL: July - September
Flower: Tiny, disk florets with slender styles. Fuzzy flower heads, rose purple, 4 to 14 in densely compacted spikes along upper part of stalks, top blossoms opening first, bloom working down along stem, feathery appearance; heads relatively small with 10 or so florets; bracts narrow, margins thin and dry.
Leaves: Numerous, linear, entire, alternate, rigid, deciduous.

256 *Liatris squarrosa* Page 182
Blazing star
LS: Perennial HT: 1 - 3 ft. BL: June - August
Flower: Bright magenta-purple disk florets; heads relatively large as in *L. scariosa*; bracts distinctively reflexed, pointed.
Leaves: Narrow, rigid, deciduous.
Habitat: (all species) Roadsides, open fields, dry open places, thin woods.
Culture: Slightly acid to neutral soil. Full sun.
Propagation: Grows from a corm or tuber, easy to transplant. Divide clumps in spring or fall. Seed germinate slowly.
Note: Attract butterflies. Species tend to hybridize making identification difficult.

23 *Parthenium integrifolium* Page 124
Wild quinine, American feverfew
LS: Perennial HT: 1 - 4 ft. BL: May - September
Flower: Receptacular bracts and short inconspicuous ray flowers surround center disk flowers making up numerous 1/4 in. heads which form a broad, flat-topped inflorescence, white and woolly.
Leaves: Alternate, ovate to lanceolate, coarsely toothed, thick and rough, upper leaves sessile, basal leaves large and long stalked.
Habitat: Dry, open woods.

Culture: Dry soil, partial shade.
Propagation: Seeds, division.

Ratibida pinnata
Gray headed coneflower
LS: Perennial HT: 2 - 3 ft. BL: June - September
Flower: Elongated disk florets (gray or brown) forming a cone, surrounded by 5 - 10 drooping yellow ray florets, head solitary, terminal, 1 - 2 in. wide.
Leaves: Compound, pinnate, deeply cut, lanceolate, leaflets 3 - 5 in. long, alternate, hairy stem.
Habitat: Dry open woods, roadsides, fencerows.
Culture: Ordinary garden soil.
Propagation: Seed or division.

116 *Rudbeckia hirta* Page 147
Black-eyed susan
LS: Perennial HT: 2 - 3 ft. BL: June - October
Flower: Showy heads with daisy like blossom, 2 - 3 in. in diameter. Yellow ray flowers with brown disk flowers which form central cone shaped head. Blooms long lasting.
Leaves: Lanceolate to oval, hairy and alternate on a slender, rough and hairy stem.
Habitat: Fields, open woods, roadsides.
Culture: Well-drained soil, slightly acid, full sun. Bushy growth habit is subject to attack by powdery mildew and aphids.
Propagation: Grown from seed which are produced freely. Sow as soon as ripe. Self seeds rapidly.

117 *Rudbeckia lacinata* Page 148
Green-headed coneflower
LS: Perennial HT: 3 - 7 ft. July - September
Flower: Yellow ray florets, reflexed; prominent greenish-yellow disc; 3 - 4 in. across.
Leaves: Pinnate, deeply lobed, toothed, thin textured.
Habitat: Open thickets, woods along streams.
Culture: Moist rich soil, full sun to light shade.
Propagation: Seeds, division.

118 *Rudbeckia triloba* Page 148
Bear's paw, Thin-leafed coneflower
LS: Perennial HT: 2 - 4 ft. BL: June - October
Flower: Daisy-like with 8 - 10 short yellow ray florets surrounding dark brown raised disk florets, up to 2 in. across. Usually several to a stem.
Leaves: Alternate, thin, rough, toothed. Lower—3 lobed 2 - 4 in. long. Upper—smaller, sessile. Branching habit.
Habitat: Open woods, fields, roadsides.
Culture: Dry or moist soil. Tolerates some shade.
Propagation: Seed sown as soon as ripe. Division.

119 *Senecio smallii* Page 148
Southern ragwort
LS: Perennial HT: 1 - 2 ft. BL: April - June

Flower: Small, golden yellow, disk and ray florets, 3/4 in., flat top clusters of 8 - 12 blooms on slender peduncles.
Leaves: Lanceolate; long stemmed basal leaves, stem leaves linear, deeply pinnately cut, stem woolly at base.
Habitat: Fields, pastures, open woods, roadsides.
Culture: Ordinary soil.
Propagation: Seed, division.

Senecio tomentosus
Woolly southern ragwort
LS: Perennial HT: 1 - 2 ft. BL: April - June
Flower: Similar to *S. smallii.*
Leaves: Lower leaves not dissected, hairy, whitish on underside and on stem.
Habitat: Sandy, rocky places, granite outcrops.
Culture: Ordinary, moist soil.
Propagation: Seed, division.

24 *Solidago bicolor* Page 124
White goldenrod, Silver-rod, Pale goldenrod
LS: Perennial HT: 1 - 3 ft. BL: July - October
Flower: Small, crowded, wandlike, ray florets white, disk florets small, yellow.
Leaves: Feather veined, alternate, toothed, small, sessile, oblong. Basal leaves stalked. Stem stiff, hairy, grayish, sometimes branched.
Habitat: Dry open woods, open fields.
Culture: Dry sandy soil, sun or semi-shade.
Propagation: By seed or division.
Note: Most goldenrods have yellow flowers (see following descriptions).

Solidago
Goldenrod
Flower: Tiny, golden yellow blossoms (both tubular and ray florets) clustered into plume-like terminal or axillary panicles. Inflorescence have distinctive shapes—plume-like (graceful), elm-branched, clublike (showy), wandlike (slender) or flat-topped.
Leaves: Large basal rosette. Others alternate. May be parallel veined (3 veins running in same direction) or feather veined (one main center vein, others radiating from it).

Solidago arguta (includes *Solidago boottii*)
Sharp-leaved goldenrod
LS: Perennial HT: 2 - 6 ft. BL: August - October
Flower: In plumelike cluster at top of stem.

120 *Solidago caesia* Page 148
Blue-stemmed goldenrod
LS: Perennial HT: 1 1/2 - 3 ft. BL: August - October
Flower: Many in clusters in upper leaf axils, wandlike.
Leaves: Lanceolate, feather veined, toothed. Stem bluish or purple with waxy bloom.

121 *Solidago canadensis* (alternatively *Solidago altissima*) Page 149
Canada goldenrod, Common field goldenrod
LS: Perennial HT: 3 - 6 ft. BL: July - September
Flower: Arranged on one side of spreading branches in a plumelike terminal cluster forming large, often loose panicle.
Leaves: Thin, lanceolate, parallel veined (triple nerved), edges sharply toothed, crowded, hairy below and rough above, long point at apex. Stem slender, smooth at base, closely downy near top.

122 *Solidago erecta* Page 149
Erect goldenrod, Slender goldenrod
LS: Perennial HT: 1 - 4 ft. BL: August - October
Flower: Yellow flower heads born in leaf axils in a tall cylindrical, terminal cluster.
Leaves: Blunt - toothed, upper leaves very small and narrow, alternate.

Solidago flexicaulis
Zigzag or Broadleaved goldenrod
LS: Perennial HT: 1 - 3 ft. BL: July - October
Flower: Small clusters in upper leaf axils and at top.
Leaves: Very broad and well pointed at both ends, feather veined. Stem angled in cross section (i.e., zigzag), rarely branched.

123 *Solidago gigantea* Page 149
Late goldenrod
LS: Perennial HT: 2 - 7 ft. BL: August - October
Flower: Plumelike inflorescence.
Leaves: Smooth with some soft hairs beneath, toothed, parallel veined. Stems smooth, pale green or purplish, often covered with whitish bloom.

124 *Solidago graminifolia* (alternatively *Euthamia graminifolia*) Page 149
Lance-leaf goldenrod
LS: Perennial HT: 1 - 4 ft. BL: July - October
Flower: Common flat top, fragrant.
Leaves: Numerous, narrow, slender and linear with 3 - 7 parallel veins, rough, untoothed, hairy edges. Stem erect.

125 *Solidago nemoralis* Page 150
Gray goldenrod
LS: Perennial HT: 1 - 3 ft. BL: August - October
Flower: Mostly a plumelike cluster, sometimes rather one-sided at top of stem.
Leaves: Rough, gray-green; smaller towards top of finely hairy stem; conspicuous tiny leaflets in leaf axils.

126 *Solidago odora* Page 150
Sweet goldenrod
LS: Perennial HT: 1 1/2 - 3 ft. BL: July - September
Flower: Plumelike
Leaves: Numerous, narrowly elliptic; anise-like odor when crushed, slender, toothless, parallel veined, show transparent dots.

127 *Solidago rigida* Page 150

Hard-leafed goldenrod

LS: Perennial HT: 1 - 5 ft. BL: August - October

Flower: Relatively large flat topped cluster.

Leaves: Extremely rigid, upper oval, sessile, clasping, broad, feather veined, thick, mostly hairy or rough on both sides. Stem hairy.

Solidago rugosa

Rough-stemmed goldenrod

LS: Perennial HT: 3 - 6 ft. BL: July - October

Flower: Resembles *S. ulmifolia*, elmbranched.

Leaves: Numerous, rough, wrinkled, harshly hairy, stems arise from narrow creeping rhizomes.

Solidago tenuifolia (alternatively *Euthamia tenuifolia*)

Slender fragrant goldenrod

LS: Perennial HT: 1 - 2 ft. BL: August - October

Flower: Flat topped, fragrant.

Leaves: Numerous, very slender, grasslike with only 1 vein, minutely dotted. Smoother and more delicate and finely cut than *S. graminifolia*. Stems slender, smooth, branched above.

128 *Solidago ulmifolia* Page 150

Elm-leafed goldenrod

LS: Perennial HT: 2 - 4 1/2 ft. BL: August - October

Flower: Elmlike cluster of several upright but arching branches near ends of stems.

Leaves: Elliptical, feather veined, thin, coarsely toothed, usually soft hairs beneath. Stem smooth and slender, flower branches hairy.

Habitat: (all species) Woods, meadows, hillsides, roadsides, fields, stream margins.

Culture: Average soil.

Propagation: Seed. Bloom 2nd year. Divide old clumps in spring. Transplant easily.

Note: Some varieties tend to be weedy. Tend to hybridize, making identification difficult. Over 85 species grow in North America. Most are yellow or gold. Goldenrod pollen is distributed by insects. It is too heavy to be borne by the wind and is not an allergen.

257 *Stokesia laevis* Page 183

Stokes aster

LS: Perennial HT: 1 - 2 ft. BL: June - July

Flower: Lavender blue or purplish, ray florets flat and fringed or toothed, disk florets tubular, growing smaller toward center, ragged appearance, 3 - 4 in. across, solitary. Surrounded by several rings of bracts more conspicuous after bloom fades.

Leaves: Dense basal rosette, lance shaped, 10 in. long, smooth, dark gray green. Stem leaves alternate, toothed, stem purplish, branching and hairy.

Habitat: Moist pine woods, roadsides, fields.

Culture: Sandy or light rich soil, full sun or light shade, good drainage.

Propagation: Seed, stem cuttings, division.

129 *Tanacetum vulgare* Page 151
Tansy, Bitter buttons, Golden buttons
LS: Perennial HT: 1 - 2 ft. BL: July - September
Flower: Yellow, small tight heads composed of all disc florets (resemble slightly rounded buttons), borne in terminal flat-topped cymes on erect stems.
Leaves: Dark green, finely cut (fernlike), alternate, compound, pinnately divided into many stalkless leaflets, toothed. Strong scent.
Habitat: Roadsides, edges of fields.
Culture: Ordinary soil.
Propagation: Seed or division.
Note: An escape from Eurasia.

258 *Vernonia noveboracensis* Page 183
Ironweed, New York ironweed
LS: Perennial HT: 3 - 7 ft. BL: August - October
Flower: Tiny, deep purple to violet, all disc florets, many grouped in thistle-like heads, heads forming loose flat-topped panicles.
Leaves: Alternate, lanceolate, pointed, upper leaves nearly sessiled, toothed, borne on stiff, erect and branching stems, hairy, 3 - 8 in. long.
Habitat: Meadows, stream banks, roadside ditches.
Culture: Moist soil, low grounds.
Propagation: Division. Seed. Self seeding.
Note: Many other Ironweeds are useful in perennial gardens where rich purples are needed in late summer to early fall.

130 *Viguiera porteri* Page 151
Stone Mountain yellow daisy, Confederate daisy
LS: Annual HT: 2 - 2 1/2 ft. BL: August - September
Flower: Yellow, 8 ray florets, dark yellow disk, 1 1/2 in. wide, extreme center darker yellow, dark brown anthers, branching habit.
Leaves: Narrow, opposite, with a cluster of long hairs where each pair joins stem.
Habitat: Shallow crevices and depressions on granite outcroppings.
Culture: Thin soil.
Propagation: Seed. Often self seeding.

Diapensia Family (*Diapensiaceae*)

Evergreen small shrubs or herbs. Flowers a 5-lobed calyx and corolla with 5 petals, 5 sepals and 5 stamens, solitary or in racemes. Leaves evergreen, simple, basal rosettes.

25 *Galax urceolata* (incorrectly formerly *Galax aphylla*) Page 125
Galax, Beetleweed
LS: Perennial HT: 4 - 12 in. BL: May - June
Flower: Tiny, white, 5-petaled, borne in a slender wand-like spike on a leafless stem.
Leaves: Evergreen, basal, lustrous, cordate, leathery, dark green turning coppery red to bronze in winter, up to 5 in. across.
Habitat: Open deciduous woods.

Culture: Acid soil, cool, slightly moist and rich peaty loam, partial shade, good drainage, mulch.
Propagation: Spreads via thick mat of runners. Divide in early spring or fall. Plant 1 in. deep. Take cuttings. Seeds minute (dust-like). Spreads rapidly.

26 *Shortia galacifolia* Page 125
Oconee bells
LS: Perennial HT: 5 - 8 in. BL: May - June
Flower: 1 in. wide, nodding, bell shaped, 5 white fringed petals, joined at base, 5 yellow stamen interspersed by 5 scales or bracts, joined to lower part of petals. Borne on leafless stalks.
Leaves: Simple, heart-shaped to ovate, form basal rosette, wavy margins, shiny, evergreen.
Habitat: Ravines, banks, woods, often beneath mountain laurel.
Culture: Moderately acid, rich humus-filled soil, shade, moisture.
Propagation: Separation of runners. Division after flowering.
Note: Endangered species.

Dogbane Family (*Apocynaceae*)

Herbs, shrubs and trees with small, nodding 5-lobed flowers with 5 united petals forming a bell-shaped bloom, borne in clusters. Leaves opposite, untoothed, simple. Exude a milky juice.

180 *Apocynum androsaemifolium* Page 163
Spreading dogbane
LS: Perennial HT: 6 - 18 in. BL: June - August
Flower: Pale pink with deeper pink stripes, 5 petals join to form a tube or bell, 3/8 in. across, numerous, borne in terminal clusters on curved stalks, fragrant.
Leaves: Opposite, ovate on short stalks.
Habitat: Thin woods, fields, roadsides.
Culture: Dry soil.
Propagation: Seed, division while dormant.

Gentian Family (*Gentianaceae*)

Annual and perennial herbs growing from rhizomes. Flowers have 4 - 5 petals and 4 - 12 sepals of variable size, joined, usually tubular at base. Leaves usually opposite, entire, simple. Fruit is a capsule with tiny seeds.

Gentiana
The gentians
Flower: Showy, solitary or clustered at the end of branches, commonly bottle-shaped, cylindrical, sometimes in leaf axils; true gentians have pleats of folded delicate tissue between the larger lobes of the petals.
Leaves: Opposite, stalkless, smooth, narrow, 1 - 2 in. long, deciduous.

Gentiana catesbaei
Catesby's gentian, Sampson's snakeroot
LS: Perennial HT: 9 - 18 in. BL: September - November
Flower: Clustered at end of stem or in leaf axils, bright deep blue, 1 in. long.
Leaves: Ovate-lanceolate, 3-nerved, margins with minute sawteeth.
Habitat: Common along riverbanks and streams in damp woods of the coastal plain.
Culture: Usually difficult, partial shade, moist soil, slightly acid to neutral.
Propagation: Seeds (form a capsule that splits open when ripe, Catch before dispersed). Usually bloom 2 - 3 years after germination. Divide old plants.

259 *Gentiana quinquefolia* Page 183
Stiff gentian, Agueweed
LS: Annual or Biennial HT: 6 - 15 in. BL:August - October
Flower: Lilac or blue, tubular, to 1 in. long, borne in tight clusters of five or more flowers at terminal end of stem and in leaf axils.
Leaves: Lance shaped to ovate, partially clasping, opposite.
Habitat: Roadsides, edges of woods, moist fields.
Culture: Rich, moist soil, partial shade, prefer high altitudes.
Propagation: Seed, division.

260 *Gentiana saponaria* Page 183
Soapwort gentian
LS: Perennial HT: 1 - 2 ft. BL: September - November
Flower: Arranged as the *G. catesbaei*, blue with white stripes or deep blue, 1 in. long, club-shaped.
Leaves: Lanceolate or oblong.
Habitat: Common in ravines and wooded slopes of the upper piedmont and mountains.
Culture: Same as *G. catesbaei*.
Propagation: Same as *G. catesbaei*.

27 *Gentiana villosa* Page 125
Pale gentian, Striped gentian, Sampson's snakeroot
LS: Perennial HT: 6 - 18 in. BL: September - October
Flower: Clustered, tubular or cylindrical, opened only slightly, greenish-white (striped within), borne on stem end or in upper leaf axils.
Leaves: 5 - 12 pairs, opposite, stalkless, smooth.
Habitat: Open woods, riverbanks.
Culture: Same as *G. catesbaei*.
Propagation: Same as *G. catesbaei*.

181 *Sabatia angularis* Page 164
Rose-pink, Bitter bloom
LS: Annual HT: 1 - 2 ft. BL: July - September
Flower: Five petals, rose pink or white, yellow eye bordered with red, 1 - 1/2 in. across, borne singly on terminal end of opposite branches giving cluster-like appearance.
Leaves: Ovate to oblong, clasping, opposite, stem angled.
Habitat: Moist fields, roadsides.
Culture: Wet soil, sun.
Propagation: Seed. Tend to hybridize with other varities making identification difficult.

Geranium Family (*Geraniaceae*)

Annual or perennial herbs, sometimes semi-woody. Flowers have 5 petals, 5 sepals, 5 - 15 stamens, borne in a cyme or umbel. Leaves deeply cleft, may be palmate or fernlike, alternate, often aromatic.

261 *Geranium maculatum* Page 184
Wild geranium, Cranesbill
LS: Perennial HT: 1 - 2 ft. BL: April - June
Flower: Loose clusters of 2 - 5, 5-petaled, pale rose-purple flowers, 1 - 1 1/2 in. wide.
Leaves: Palmately cleft into 5-7 toothed lobes, hairy, gray-green, long stemmed at base—short stemmed, opposite higher on main stem.
Habitat: Slightly moist, rich woods, shady roadsides, meadows.
Culture: Sun or light shade, sheltered, protect from wind, slightly acid to neutral soil.
Propagation: Rhizome division in spring or fall. Seeds sown as soon as ripe. Seedlings bloom in 2 - 3 years. Easily grown—readily adapts to cultivation.
Note: Common name comes from long-beaked seed pod which resembles a crane's bill.

Heath Family (*Ericaceae*)

Shrubs and small trees. Flowers have 4 - 5 sepals and petals, usually united in a bell-shaped form, 8 - 10 stamens, solitary or in racemes. Mostly deciduous although some are evergreen.

182 *Epigaea repens* Page 164
Trailing arbutus, Mayflower
LS: Perennial HT: 6 in. BL: March - May
Flower: 5 - 6 terminal and axillary clusters, pale pink to white, tubular, about 1/2 in. wide, flaring into 5 lobes. Very fragrant.
Leaves: Oval, blunt or pointed at tip, heart shaped at base, leathery, evergreen, 1 - 3 in. long, alternate. Prostrate—trailing hairy stems spread on the ground forming dense mats.
Habitat: Deciduous or coniferous woods.
Culture: Cool conditions, leafy mold, sandy, rocky or peaty soil, semi-shade, very acid soil. A fungus inhabits the roots and must be present in the soil for successful cultivation.
Propagation: By seed or by stem-layering. Seedlings take 3 years to flower. Not easy to cultivate. Best to attempt to move only small plants and then only when it is threatened.
Note: Although technically a woody plant, most gardeners regard trailing arbutus as a spring wildflower.

Evening Primrose Family (*Onagraceae*)

Herbs and some shrubs (some aquatic). Flowers large, showy, 4 petals, 4 sepals, 4 - 8 stamens, 4 branched stigma forms a cross, borne in leaf axils or terminal racemes. Close after midday. Leaves simple, alternate or opposite.

131 *Oenothera biennis* Page 151

Evening primrose, Needles and thread, Evening star

LS: Biennial HT: 1 - 4 ft. BL: June - September

Flower: Pale yellow, large, somewhat tubular, 1 - 2 in. wide, 4 broad petals, 4 reflexed sepals, 8 stamen. Fragrant—lemon scented. Arise from axils of upper leaflike bracts forming loose spikes. Each blossom lasts one day. New blooms appear until fall. Erect oval fruits cluster along upper stem releasing seeds periodically.

Leaves: Only has flat basal leaves with white mid-vein in the first year, 4 - 8 in., lanceolate, slightly toothed, alternate, hairy, smaller than basal leaves, stalkless. Stem stout and hairy, sometimes tinged with purple, usually branching near top.

Habitat: Fields, roadsides, open places.

Culture: Dry or sandy soil, well drained, full sun. Tends to be aggressive.

Propagation: Seed (capsule urn-shaped). Self seeding. Transplant seedlings.

Note: Good source of bird food—especially for goldfinch. Said to attract Japanese beetles from other plants.

132 *Oenothera fruticosa* Page 151

Sundrops

LS: Perennial HT: 1 - 3 ft. BL: May - August

Flower: Four petals, cup-shaped, slender calyx tube arising from a swollen ovary, bright yellow, orange stamens, 1 - 2 in. wide, loose clusters arising from leaf axils. Strongly ribbed pods or capsules are club-shaped and 1/2 in. long. Day blooming—open in the sunshine.

Leaves: Lance shaped, plain edged, alternate, spotted with purple, hairy; the stems are heavily branched and tend to sprawl.

Habitat: Meadows, fields, open places.

Culture: Light dry sandy soil, full sun, slightly acid.

Propagation: Seed, stem cuttings. Division every 2 - 3 years.

Note: Taxonomy of sundrops is confusing. Although most horticultural references refer to one species, there are, in fact, many in nature. Sundrops are particularly good outcrop plants. If capsules are oblong and have glandular hairs, *Oenothera tetragona* may be recognized.

183 *Oneothera speciosa* Page 164

Showy evening primrose, Windflower

LS: Perennial* HT: 6 - 15 in. BL: May - July

Flower: White, pale pink or white with pink lines, 4 broad- notched petals, 8 stamens, yellow anthers, bowl-shaped, borne in upper leaf axils, 3 in. wide. Buds nod. Opens in the evening, blooms fully the next morning.

Leaves: 2 - 3 in. long, linear to ovate, wavy margins, alternate. Stems slender and downy.

Habitat: Roadsides, railroad banks, fields.

Culture: Dry, light sandy soil, well drained, full sun.

Propagation: Seed, division. Colonizes by running rhizomes and prolific seeds. Tends to be weedy.

Note: Native in southern prairie states, but often naturalized along our roadsides.

* Sometimes an annual in north Georgia.

Forget-me-not Family (*Boraginaceae*)

Annual or perennial herbs, shrubs and trees. Flowers expand from a one-sided rolled up coil, gradually unfolding with growth. Usually 5 united petals form tubular corolla, borne in cymes or racemes. Leaves alternate, undivided, hairy, entire.

296 *Mertensia virginica* Page 192
Virginia bluebells, Cowslip
LS: Perennial HT: 10 - 20 in. BL: April - May
Flower: Bell-shaped, 1 in. long, pinkish in bud, blue when older, borne in short, nodding racemes.
Leaves: Upper: Gray-green, oval, smooth, sessile, alternate, strong veins. Basal. Ovate. Deciduous.
Habitat: Bottomlands, open moist deciduous woods, along streams.
Culture: Semi-shade, moist humus-filled soil, calcareous or neutral to basic. Leaves dry up early in the year—do not cut off.
Propagation: Seed. Flower 3rd year. Difficult to divide—dig very deep to be sure you get the bulb as it tends to work down in the soil. Difficult to maintain without proper soils rich in lime.

Four o'clock Family (*Nyctaginaceae*)

Herbs, woody vines, shrubs or trees. Flowers without petals in small clusters above green 5 part joined bracts resembling a calyx. Leaves simple.

133 *Mirabilia jalapa* Page 152
Four o'clock, Beauty-of-the-night
LS: Perennial* HT: 1 - 3 ft. BL: July - September
Flower: Large, funnel or trumpet shaped, 1 - 2 in. wide. Red, pink, yellow, white or purple. Open in late afternoon. Fragrant.
Leaves: Heart shaped, opposite, 2 - 3 in. wide, dark green. Bushy habit.
Habitat: Waste places, old homesteads.
Culture: Full sun or partial shade, well aerated soil, good drainage.
Propagation: Seed. Division of tubers (resemble potatoes). Dig deep. Tends to be aggressive.
Note: An escape from West Indies

*May be grown as an annual in Georgia.

Iris Family (*Iridaceae*)

Perennial, non-woody herbaceous plants, growing from corms, rhizomes or bulbs. Showy flowers with 3 petals, 3 sepals, 3 stamens, 3 styles (irregular in Iris—3 falls, 3 standards, 3 prominent styles). Leaves flat, swordlike, mostly basal.

165 *Belamcanda chinensis* Page 160
Blackberry lily
LS: Perennial HT: 1 - 3 ft. BL: June - August
Flower: Red, spotted orange, 6 petaled (lasts only one day). Several blooms usually open at once. Capsule splits upon becoming dry exposing shiny blackberry-like seeds. Flower 1 - 1 1/2 in. across.
Leaves: Narrow, flat, sword like, rising from a basal cluster.
Habitat: Roadsides, open woods, fields.
Culture: Hardy and drought resistant, ordinary soil.
Propagation: Seed or division.

Iris
Iris
Flower: Distinctive, 3 erect petals (standards) and 3 larger petal-like sepals (falls) marked with crests or a contrasting color.
Leaves: Simple, alternate, overlapping, flat, sword-shaped.

262 *Iris cristata* Page 184
Crested dwarf iris
LS: Perennial HT: 4 - 6 in. BL: April - May
Flower: Single, light violet with fringed orange and white crests.
Leaves: Flat, lanceolate, arching toward tip, overlapping on flower stem.
Habitat: Rich deciduous woods, ravines, bluffs, wooded hillsides, stream banks.
Culture: Soil barely acid, well drained to moist, half to full sun.
Propagation: (all species) Seed. Bloom 3rd year. Divide clumps after flowering. Leave a feeding root on leaf fan and rhizome. Transplant rhizome after blooming. Plant close to surface.

134 *Iris pseudacorus* Page 152
Yellow iris
LS: Perennial HT: 1 - 3 ft. BL: May - June
Flower: Yellow standards and falls.
Leaves: Flat, swordlike and upright.
Habitat: Marshes, stream banks.
Culture: Slightly acid to neutral soil.
Propagation: Same as *I. cristata*.
Note: Only found naturalized in Georgia. Apparently originally introduced from western Europe or North Africa.

263 *Iris verna* Page 184
Vernal iris
LS: Perennial HT: 3 in. BL: April - May
Flower: Fragrant, lavender blue with no crests. Yellow or orange smooth bands on sepals (falls).
Leaves: Flat, narrow and long (6 - 8 in.).
Habitat: Deciduous or coniferous woody hillsides, drier woods than *I. cristata*.
Culture: Intensely acid, well-drained soil. Difficult to grow.
Propagation: Same as *I. cristata*.
Note: Smallest of native iris.

264 *Iris versicolor* Page 184

Blue flag

LS: Perennial HT: 2 - 3 ft. BL: June - July

Flower: Violet blue with yellow based sepals. Several borne on erect stem.

Leaves: Thick, blade like.

Habitat: Wet meadows, marshes.

Culture: Slightly acid to neutral soil, moist.

Propagation: Same as *I. cristata*.

297 *Sisyrinchium angustifolium* Page 193

Blue-eyed grass

LS: Perennial HT: 4 - 12 in. BL: May - June

Flower: Dainty, blue, pointed, 3 petals and 3 sepals with yellow center or "eye", small, 1/2 in. wide. Bloom lasts only one day.

Leaves: Flattened, narrow and grasslike, iris-like in arrangement (stem seems to merge with leaves).

Habitat: Moist fields, meadows.

Culture: Sun, moist, well drained slightly acid to neutral soil.

Propagation: Seed sown as soon as ripe (in late summer). Division of root segments.

Lily Family (*Liliaceae*)

Mostly herbs growing from bulbs, corms or rhizomes; some succulents and woody-stemmed vines. Perennials. Flowers large and showy, bell like or triangular with 3 sepals, 3 petals, 6 stamens; often petals indistinguishable from sepals and then all 6 are called tepals. Leaves parallel-veined, basal, alternate or in whorls.

28 *Amianthium muscaetoxicum* Page 125

Fly poison

LS: Perennial HT: 1 - 3 ft. BL: May - July

Flower: White, small, 3 petals and 3 petal-like sepals, in dense terminal cylindrical clusters, 2 - 6 in. long. Turns yellow-green to green with age. Bracts at base of flower stalks slightly cupped at tips.

Leaves: Numerous, grasslike, mostly basal, v-shaped ribs, up to 2 ft. long.

Habitat: Open woods, bogs.

Culture: Light sandy soil, sun, acid.

Propagation: Seeds, division.

Note: Poisonous.

265 *Camassia scilloides* Page 185

Wild hyacinth

LS: Perennial HT: 3 - 15 in. BL: May - June

Flower: Pale blue, blue-violet or white, 6 pointed segments, star-shaped, 1/2 in. wide, in an elongated, loose flower cluster.

Leaves: Linear, grasslike, keeled, basal.

Habitat: Meadows, open woods.

Culture: Neutral, ordinary garden soil, sun or partial shade, moisture.
Propagation: Division of bulbs after foliage ripens. Seeds take 3 - 4 years to reach flowering size.

Clintonia borealis
Bluebead lily, Yellow wood lily, Corn lily
LS: Perennial HT: 8 - 16 in. BL: May - June
Flower: Bell shaped, 6 segments, up to 1 in. long, nodding, forming a loose umbel at top of stem. Pale greenish-yellow. Blue berries in fall.
Leaves: Basal, broad, 4 - 8 in. long, arranged usually in threes, oval, lustrous dark green, sheathing base of stem.

Clintonia umbellulata
Speckled wood lily, Clinton's lily
LS: Perennial HT: 8 - 20 in. BL: May - June
Flower: White, often dotted green or purple, bell shaped, up to 1/2 in. long, borne in tight upright rounded clusters at tip of downy stalk. Not nodding. Fragrant. Produces blue bead-like berries in fall.
Leaves: Same as *C. borealis*.
Habitat: (both species) Moist woods, thickets.
Culture: Cool, rich, moist humus-filled soil, shade, acid, good drainage.
Propagation: Seed (remove pulp). Plant as soon as ripe. Bloom in 2 - 3 years. Division in fall. Spread by long rhizomes or underground stems. When transplanting take underground runner and bud for following year's growth.
Note: *C. borealis* normally prefers spruce-fir or northern hardwoods and reaches Georgia only on our highest mountains.

29 *Chamaelirium luteum* Page 126
Fairy wand, Devil's bit
LS: Perennial HT: 1 - 3 ft. BL: April - June
Flower: Numerous, small, white, tightly packed on a wand-like 3 - 9 in. spike, sometimes drooping at tip. Male and female flowers on separate plants; female plants are less frequent and become much more robust when in fruit (a tiny, many seeded capsule).
Leaves: Smooth, narrow and pointed, alternate along stem, basal rosette leaves obovate, obtuse, larger.
Habitat: Upland woodlands, meadows. Basal rosettes commonly seen in upland woods.
Culture: Moderately rich soil, moist, partial shade.
Propagation: Seed, division.

30 *Convallaria majalis* Page 126
Lily of the valley
LS: Perennial HT: 6 - 9 in. BL: April - May
Flower: White, bell shaped, fragrant. Inflorescence one sided on stem, higher than leaves.
Leaves: 2 - 3 strongly veined, deciduous. Flowering stems sheathed on lower part of leaf. Plants eventually form large mats.
Note: An escape from Europe. Naturalized occasionally.

31 *Convallaria montana* Page 126

Wild lily of the valley

LS: Perennial HT: 6 - 9 in. BL: April - May

Flower: White with green stripes, not fragrant; inflorescence shorter than the leaves.

Leaves: Same as *C. majalis* except plants are widely scattered in small clumps.

Habitat: (Both species) Clearings, light woods.

Culture: Partial shade, ordinary soil, slightly acid.

Propagation: Seed or division.

Note: Native to North Georgia mountains. Often confused with *C. majalis.*

135 *Erythronium americanum* and *Erythronium umbilicatum* Page 152

Trout lily, Adder's tongue, Dog tooth violet, Fawn lily

LS: Perennial HT: 5 - 10 in. BL: March - May

Flower: Solitary, yellow, often spotted at base, nodding, about 1 1/2 in. long, with 3 petals and 3 sepals curved backward in a lily-like manner. Borne on stalk that arises between leaves.

Leaves: Basal, green mottled with purplish-brown and white streaks, elliptical, deciduous. When plant is young it has a single leaf; two appear later.

Habitat: Moist deciduous or mixed woodlands, thickets, along banks and slopes.

Culture: Rich, deep loam, light shade or full sun, acid to neutral soil. Mulch with chopped leaves.

Propagation: By offshoots. Separate and plant immediately either in summer or fall. By seed when ripe. Plant both shoots and seeds 3 - 5 in. deep. Plants grown from seed may take 3 - 5 years to bloom. Small bulbs are deep seated. Be sure to dig deep when moving since bulb tends to work its way down into the soil. Tends to colonize.

Note: Georgia has two species of yellow trout lilies, very difficult to tell apart unless in fruit. The fruit of *E. americanum* has a dimple at its apex; this species is found in north Georgia mountains. The fruit of *E. umbilicatum* has a small beak at its apex; this species reaches beech forests of South Georgia.

166 *Hemerocallis fulva* Page 160

Tawny day lily, Common day lily

LS: Perennial HT: 2 - 4 ft. BL: June - July

Flower: Tawny orange, funnel shaped, corolla opening for only one day, 3 petals, 3 sepals, up to 5 in. in diameter. Held upright on leafless flower scape. Usually several blooms per plant.

Leaves: Basal, narrow and swordlike, tapering to acute tip, spreading, 1 - 2 ft. long.

Habitat: Meadows, along streams and roadsides.

Culture: Well-drained soil, otherwise not fussy.

Propagation: Spreads rapidly by stolons or rhizomes. Divide in August or September. Rarely seeds.

Note: An escape from Eurasia, naturalized throughout Georgia. Both common and botanical name derived from flowering habit and means "beautiful for a day".

136 *Lilium canadense* Page 152

Canada lily, Fairy caps

LS: Perennial HT: 2 - 5 ft. BL: June - July

Flower: One or more nodding bell-shaped flowers 2 - 3 in., color range yellow to orange red with dark spots; petals and sepals arch outward (not back).

Leaves: Regularly whorled along erect stem, lanceolate to narrowly elliptic, with fine sawtooth margins (very minute teeth).
Habitat: Rich woodlands, borders.
Culture: Soil reasonably fertile, slightly acid, part shade.
Propagation: By scales found on bulbs.

167 *Lilium lancifolium* (formerly called *Lilium tigrinum*) Page 160
Tiger lily
LS: Perennial HT: 2 - 5 ft. BL: June - August
Flower: Orange, heavily spotted with purplish brown dots, tips of petals and sepals recurving, nearly 5 in. wide, nodding (does not have green center).
Leaves: Alternate, lanceolate, dark bulbits in axils.
Habitat: Meadows, roadsides and thickets.
Culture: Acid, loamy humus-filled soil, sun or partial shade.
Propagation: By scales, seeds or bulbits (takes patience). Bloom in 2 - 4 years. Move in fall to allow to become re-established before spring. Plant at least 5 in. deep.
Note: An escape from the Far East.

Lilium michauxii
Carolina lily
LS: Perennial HT: 1 - 3 ft. BL: June - August
Flower: Orange-red, dotted brown. Petals and sepals sharply reflexed, nodding. Smaller than Turk's cap and less floriferous (1 - 3 flowers per plant).
Leaves: Bluish-green, whorled, thick, broadest toward tip.
Habitat: Dry upland woods (oak-pine), along edges of woods and banks.
Culture: Acid, loamy, humus-filled soil, partial or full shade.
Propagation: Division.

168 *Lilium philadelphicum* Page 160
Wood lily
LS: Perennial HT: 1 - 3 ft. BL: June - August
Flower: Brilliant orange to red, spotted purple-brown, 3 petals and 3 petal-like sepals, each taperd into a narrow, clawed base, cup or funnel shaped, upward facing, 2 - 4 in. wide, borne terminally on stem.
Leaves: Whorled, lance-shaped (3 - 8) per whorl, 1 - 3 in. long.
Habitat: Wet meadows, wood openings.
Culture: Sandy acid soil, sun or light shade.
Propagation: Seed sown as soon as ripe, scales removed from bulbs after flowering, division.

169 *Lilium superbum* Page 161
Turk's cap lily
LS: Perennial HT: 3 - 6 ft. BL: July - September
Flower: Showy, orange spotted purple-brown, 3 petals and 3 sepals completely reflexed (forming the turk's cap), center green star shaped, 2 - 5 in. long stamens with brown anthers. Flowers borne singly or in pairs on a long pedicel and hang with anthers downward. Very profuse bloomer.
Leaves: Lance shaped to narrowly elliptic, whorled, with smooth margins.
Habitat: Moist meadows, damp thin woods, low lying areas.

Culture: Rich, loamy, humus-filled soil, acidic, sun or semi-shade. Good drainage.
Propagation: Division.

32 *Maianthemum canadense* Page 126
False lily of the valley, Canada mayflower
LS: Perennial HT: 3 - 6 in. BL: March - June
Flower: White, 4 pointed petals, in terminal spike or racemes 1 - 2 in. long. Clusters of red berries in the late summer.
Leaves: Two or 3, ovate, nearly heart-shaped at base, glossy, deciduous. Stems zigzag.
Habitat: Rich woods.
Culture: Rich acidic soil, shade or semi-shade.
Propagation: Division. Easily transplanted. Fast growing, makes thick colonies.

137 *Medeola virginiana* Page 153
Indian cucumber root
LS: Perennial HT: 12 - 18 in. BL: May - June
Flower: Small, 1/2 in. wide, greenish-yellow, 6 segments with reflexed tips, long reddish stamens. Dangles below the top leaves, 2 - 9 per plant. Blue berries in the fall.
Leaves: Two whorls, 3 - 5 at top, 5 - 9 nearer middle of stem, oblong, pointed, close to stem. Leaves at top 1 - 2 in. long, leaves at middle 2 - 4 in. long.
Habitat: Woods.
Culture: Moist soil, rich humus, moderately acid, shade.
Propagation: By seed sown as soon as ripe. Division.

266 *Muscari botryoides* Page 185
Grape hyacinth
LS: Perennial HT: 4 - 10 in. BL: April - May
Flower: Small, ball-like flowers, clustered in a terminal spike-like raceme on leafless flowering stalk, deep blue or purple, rarely white.
Leaves: Narrow, elongated, basal.
Habitat: Fields, roadsides.
Culture: Light loam
Propagation: Seeds, offsets, division.
Note: An escape from Europe.

33 *Ornithogalum umbellatum* Page 127
Star-of-Bethlehem
LS: Perennial HT: 6 - 12 in. BL: May - June
Flower: Six petals, pointed, white with greenish stripe on the underside, 1 in. wide, yellow anthers. Borne in umbels on upright stem. Opens only in the sun (not on cloudy days). Closes in the early afternoon.
Leaves: Narrow, grasslike, smooth, whitish midrib. Deciduous.
Habitat: Fields, roadsides.
Culture: Sun or semi-shade, ordinary soil.
Propagation: Division of offsets from bulbs when dormant.
Note: An escape from Europe and North Africa. Often aggressive.

34 *Polygonatum biflorum* Page 127

Soloman's seal

LS: Perennial HT: 1 - 3 ft. BL: April - May

Flower: Pendant and bell-shaped, greenish white, 1/4 - 1/2 in. long, grow from base or axil of leaves, usually in pairs. Fruit dark blue berries.

Leaves: Elliptical, 2 - 4 in. long, alternate, close to stem, parallel veined, deciduous. Stem slender and arching, unbranched.

Habitat: Dry to moist woods, coniferous or deciduous.

Culture: Partial to deep shade, humus rich soil, acidic.

Propagation: Divide thick, creeping rhizome in spring. Transplant when dormant. Sow seed in fall. Flower in 2 - 4 years. Self seeding.

35 *Smilacina racemosa* Page 127

False Solomon's seal

LS: Perennial HT: 8 - 15 in. BL: April - June

Flower: Small, 1/4 in. wide, white or creamy, clustered in loose, feathery raceme at the ends of the stem which zigzags from leaf to leaf. Red berries in the fall.

Leaves: Oval and pointed, conspicuous ribs, alternate, sessile, deciduous. Stem slightly arching.

Habitat: Moist woods, rocky slopes, under shrubs and low trees.

Culture: Light shade, acid and well-drained soil.

Propagation: By root division, leaving 1 or more eyes on each section. By seed (separate from pulp) as soon as ripened in fall. Germinate in 2 years, bloom in 5. Plant just below the soil surface. Transplant in spring or fall.

Trillium

Trillium

Easy to identify to genus. All parts are in threes or multiples of 3—3 leaves, 3 sepals, 3 petals, 3 stigmas, 6 stamens. Trillium is derived from the Latin "tri" meaning three.

184 *Trillium catesbaei* Page 164

Catesby's trillium, Rose trillium

LS: Perennial HT: 8 - 20 in. BL: April - June

Flower: Single, terminal, nodding, pink or white. Dangles below leaves. Center is white with deep yellow, twisted anthers.

Leaves: Three, triangular, whorled.

220 *Trillium cuneatum* Page 173

Whippoorwill flower

LS: Perennial HT: 8 - 20 in. BL: April - June

Flower: Single, terminal, red, looks partially open, spicy fragrance.

Leaves: Mottled, green, triangular, whorled, just below flower.

36, *Trillium erectum* Pages 127, 174

221 Wakerobin, Stinking Benjamin

LS: Perennial HT: 7 - 16 in. BL: April - June

Flower: Single, terminal, maroon or purple, sometimes white or yellow, erect above leaves. Unpleasant odor. Centers are dark. Blooms when robins return to the north.

Leaves: Three, triangular, whorled.

37 *Trillium grandiflorum* Page 128
Large flowered or White trillium
LS: Perennial HT: 12 - 18 in. BL: April - June
Flower: Single, terminal, 3 showy petals, trumpet-flaring, white turning pink with age. Held above leaves by peduncle. Centers are white with yellow anthers. Showiest trillium and easiest to grow.
Leaves: Three broad triangular, entire, whorled, just below flower.

138 *Trillium luteum* Page 153
Yellow trillium
LS: Perennial HT: 8 - 20 in. BL: April - June
Flower: Single, terminal, greenish yellow, looks partially open, lemony fragrance.
Leaves: Mottled green, whorled.

38 *Trillium rugelii* Page 128
Southern nodding trillium
LS: Perennial HT: 10 - 18 in. BL: April - June
Flower: Single, terminal (drooping or nodding), white (rarely pink), dangles below leaves; centers are white with purple anthers.
Leaves: Three, triangular, green, whorled.

39 *Trillium undulatum* Page 128
Painted trillium
LS: Perennial HT: 8 - 20 in. BL: April - June
Flower: Single, terminal, red blaze or inverted pink "V" at the base of each white, wavy edged petal.
Leaves: Three, triangular, whorled, just below flower.

222 *Trillium vaseyi* Page 174
Vasey's trillium
LS: Perennial HT: 8 - 20 in. BL: April - June
Flower: Dark maroon—purple, yellow anthers, 3 - 4 in. across (biggest trillium), dangles below leaves.
Leaves: Three, large, green.
Habitat: (all species) Mixed deciduous and evergreen woods.
Culture: (all species) Rich woods, neutral to slightly acid. Peaty, humus-filled soil, light to full shade. Most are easily grown and long lived. *T. undulatum*, the hardest to grow, prefers deep shade and acid soil.
Propagation: Seed sown when ripe. Flower in 5 - 7 years. Divide clumps when dormant. Transplant at any time, taking sufficient ball of soil. Late summer or early fall best time to move. When planting cover rhizomes with about 2 in. of soil. Do not pick. Rootstalks die if leaves and flowers are removed.

139 *Uvularia grandiflora* Page 153
Large flowered bellwort, Big merrybells
LS: Perennial HT: 15 - 20 in. BL: April - June
Flower: Large, narrow, bell shaped, drooping from ends of forked stem, single, bright lemon yellow, 1 - 1 1/2 in. long, smooth inside.
Leaves: Perfiolate, oblong, alternate, hairy below. Deciduous.

140 *Uvularia perfoliata* Page 153

Woods merrybells

LS: Perennial HT: 8 - 15 in. BL: April - June

Flower: Drooping, pale yellow, solitary, graceful, 1 1/2 in. long, fragrant, rough inside.

Leaves: Perfoliate, lance-shaped, dark green, parallel veined. Stem forked. Deciduous.

141 *Uvularia sessilifolia* Page 154

Merrybells, Little bellwort, Wild oats

LS: Perennial HT: 8 - 10 in. BL: April - June

Flower: Creamy yellow, narrow, bell shaped, divided in 6 segments, tips somewhat spreading, 1 in. long, usually 2 drooping from ends of forked stem.

Leaves: Sessile, oblong, alternate, pale green above, whitish below. Deciduous.

Habitat: (all species) Rich deciduous woods, thickets.

Culture: (all species) Shade, moist but well drained rich and peaty soil, neutral to acid.

Propagation: By division in late fall. Grow from underground stems or thick creeping rootstock. Seeds sown in fall require freezing for germination.

40 *Yucca filamentosa* Page 128

Bear grass, Adam's needle

LS: Perennial HT: 3 - 6 ft. BL: June - November

Flower: Greenish to creamy white, drooping, bell shaped, about 1 1/2 in. wide, 3 petals, 3 sepals, borne in a loose terminal panicle up to 1 foot long on a woody central stalk.

Leaves: Basal rosette, tall and narrow, gray-green, rigid, loose curly threads on leaf margins. Evergreen.

Habitat: Dunes, pine barrens, fields, bluffs, roadsides, railroad banks.

Culture: Full or partial sun, sandy soil, rich, well drained, fibrous, acid to neutral.

Propagation: Spread by offsets. Division of crowns in spring or fall. Seed.

Note: Two other species of *Yucca* are commonly cultivated in Georgia and are also found on sand dunes in nature. *Yucca aloifolia*, Spanish bayonet, has rough-edged stiff leaves ending in a sharp point. *Yucca gloriosa*, Spanish dagger or Roman candle, has smooth leaves with a stiff terminal point; sometimes this species has a 6 - 8 ft. high trunk.

Logania Family (*Loganiaceae*)

Shrubs, trees or herbs. Regular, 4 - 5 lobed calyx and corolla, flowers borne in panicles, cymes or heads, rarely solitary. Leaves opposite, simple.

223 *Spigelia marilandica* Page 174

Indian pink, Pinkroot

LS: Perennial HT: 1 - 2 ft. BL: March - June

Flower: Red, trumpet shaped flower with 5 sharp-pointed petals at end of trumpet, forming a yellow star.

Leaves: 2 - 4 in. long, opposite, ovate.

Habitat: Moist rich woods, damp clearings.

Culture: Prefers limestone soil.

Propagation: Seed, division.

Meadow Beauty Family (*Melastomataceae*)

Mainly tropical. Genus *Rhexia* has 4 petals, 4 sepals, 8 stamens. Leaves opposite, linear veined.

185 *Rhexia virginica* Page 165
Virginia Meadow-beauty, Deergrass, Handsome Harry
LS: Perennial HT: 1 - 2 ft. BL: July - September
Flower: 4 broadly rounded ovate petals, 1 - 1 1/2 in. across, deep vivid rose-pink, 8 prominent yellow stamens sharply bent down, borne in branched terminal cymes, petals drop in afternoon; fruit an urn-shaped capsule with 4 points.
Leaves: Ovate to lanceolate, slightly toothed, rounded at base, 3/4 - 2 in. long, 3 - 5 prominent veins, opposite, nearly sessile; square, slightly winged stem.
Habitat: Creek banks, bogs, marshes, wet open woods.
Culture: Moist, sandy or peaty soil, acid, full sun or partial shade.
Propagation: Seed sown in fall, cuttings in early summer, division of tubers in spring or fall.

Milkweed Family (*Asclepiadaceae*)

Perennial herbs, vines or shrubs, occasionally succulents. Flowers have 5 swept-back petals, an inner crown resembling a 5-parted cup, borne in umbel-like clusters. Leaves alternate, paired or in whorls of 4, simple, entire, stipulate. Exudes thick usually milky juice.

186 *Asclepias amplexicaulis* Page 165
Curly milkweed, Blunt-leaved milkweed
LS: Perennial HT: 2 - 4 ft. BL: March - September
Flower: Five hood-like lobes, generally reflexed, greenish suffused with magenta-purple or rose, numerous, in a terminal umbel up to 2 - 3 in. across.
Leaves: Simple, sessile, ovate to oblong-lanceolate, broad and blunt, wavy margined, waxy, opposite, exudes thick milky juice, long and slender pointed seedpod.
Habitat: Thin woods, open areas, meadows, roadsides.
Culture: Dry sandy soil.
Propagation: Seeds, division.

170 *Asclepias tuberosa* Page 161
Butterfly weed, Chigger weed, Pleurisy root
LS: Perennial HT: 1 - 2 ft. BL: June - August
Flower: Small, brilliant orange in terminal flat clusters.
Leaves: Oblong-ovate, almost sessile, hairy, alternate on stout, rough, hairy stems. Juice watery and not milky as in other members of milkweed family.
Habitat: Roadsides, open fields, light woods.
Culture: Well-drained, dry soil. Full or lightly filtered sun. Grows from rhizome with long taproot. Clumps 1 - 2 ft. wide. Late to break dormancy. Longer bloom period encouraged by pruning back.
Propagation: Seedpod spindle shaped. Gather seed when completely dry. Seeds slow to

germinate. Long and brittle taproot is easily broken and makes transplanting difficult. If attempted, do so while dormant and only attempt to dig small plants. Give a permanent spot in the garden.
Note: Plant scarce in some areas due to construction activities and the considerable time required for establishment of new populations. Attracts multitudes of butterflies.

Milkwort Family (*Polygalaceae*)

Herbs, shrubs, small trees and vines. Flowers irregular, tiny, borne in crowded heads, 5 sepals (2 winged, 3 smaller and united in a tube, lower one may be crested), 3 tiny united petals, 1 pistil. Leaves usually alternate, small, linear, simple.

267 *Polygala curtissii* Page 185
Curtiss milkwort
LS: Annual HT: 4 - 12 in. BL: June - October
Flower: Five sepals, 3 petals, joined with each other and with stamens, rose-purple tipped pale yellow, borne in terminal closely packed cylindrical racemes resembling clover heads, 1/2 in. across.
Leaves: Alternate, linear.
Habitat: Granite outcroppings, thin to normal pinelands, roadsides.
Culture: Sandy or rocky dry soil.
Propagation: Seed.

187 *Polygala polygama* Page 165
Racemed milkwort
LS: Perennial HT: 5 - 7 in. BL: May - June
Flower: Pink or rose, very tiny, in loose slender raceme, never opens.
Leaves: Attached singly, alternate, linear, profuse, branching.
Habitat: Fields, thin open woods.
Culture: Sandy ordinary soil.
Propagation: Division of underground runners. Does not seed at flower.
Note: This is especially common in the Piedmont area; there are many other milkworts worthy of experimentation in the garden.

Mint Family (*Labiatae*)

Herbs and shrubs. Flowers usually small. Tubed corolla with 2 flaring lips, upper lip notched or 2 lobed, lower lip 3 lobed, in spikes or clusters borne in leaf axils. Leaves opposite, simple, often aromatic, square-stemmed.

298 *Ajuga reptans* Page 193
Bugleweed
LS: Perennial HT: 4 - 8 in. BL: May - July
Flower: Dark blue, corolla has short upper lip and pronounced 3 lobed lower lip. Borne in leafy terminal spike 2 - 4 in. long.

Leaves: Opposite, ovate, wavy. Bronze or purple beneath. Square stem.
Habitat: Fields, roadsides.
Culture: Sun, semi-shade.
Propagation: Seed. Division. Spreads by low creeping runners forming dense beds.
Note: An escape from Europe.

41 *Collinsonia serotina* Page 129
Horse-balm, Stoneroot
LS: Perennial HT: 1 - 2 ft. BL: July - October
Flower: White, corolla irregular, 1/2 - 3/4 in. long, 5 petals fused into two lips, upper lip three toothed, long lower lip fringed, borne in branched terminal racemes 4 - 6 in. long, 4 stamens, anise scented.
Leaves: Opposite, ovate, 4 - 6 in. long, anise scented when crushed.
Habitat: Rich woods.
Culture: Rich humus-filled moist soil, shade.
Propagation: Seeds, division.

Monarda
Bee balm, Oswego tea, Bergamot
Flower: 2 lipped corolla, elongated, borne in clusters, partially concealed by showy colored bracts, ragged appearance.
Leaves: Ovate to lanceolate, aromatic, opposite. Square stem.

188 *Monarda citriodora* Page 165
Lemon mint, Horse mint
LS: Perennial HT: 1 - 2 ft. BL: June - July
Flower: White or pink dotted with light purple spots, long and narrow, two lipped; upper lip arched, lower broader lip turns down, up to 1 1/2 in. across; grouped in a dense head at terminal end of square stem with similar clusters in axils below; downy bracts form cup around flower and taper to long sharp tips.
Leaves: Lanceolate to oblong, toothed, up to 2 in. long, opposite.
Habitat: Moist areas in open woods or fields.
Culture: Sandy limestone soil, sun or partial shade.
Propagation: Seeds, cuttings, division (in spring).

224 *Monarda didyma* Page 174
Bee balm, Oswega tea
LS: Perennial HT: 2 - 3 ft. BL: June - August
Flower: Bright red, bracts tinged with red, 2 - 3 in. dense rounded heads.
Leaves: Ovate, 3 - 6 in. long, hairy beneath, dark green, tinged red at flowers.
Habitat: Along streams, damp deciduous woods and meadows.
Culture: Rich, wet acid soil. Cutting back after blooming keeps plant compact and encourages further blooming.
Propagation: (all species) Sow seeds in spring or fall. Divide clumps often, in spring.
Note: Attracts bees and butterflies.

Monarda fistulosa
Wild bergamot
LS: Perennial HT: 2 - 3 ft. BL: June - August
Flower: Purple, clustered, bracts white or purple.
Leaves: Lanceolate, hairy, light green on slender stem.
Habitat: Dry waysides, fence rows, sunny slopes.
Culture: Sandy soil, nearly neutral.
Propagation: Same as *M. didyma*.

Monarda punctata
Horsemint
LS: Perennial HT: 2 - 3 ft. BL: June - August
Flower: In whorls, lilac, bracts white to lilac.
Leaves: Hairy, lanceolate.
Habitat: Dry waysides, fence rows, sunny slopes.
Culture: Sandy soil, nearly neutral.
Propagation: Same as *M. didyma*.

268 *Physostegia virginiana* Page 185
False dragonhead, Obedient plant
LS: Perennial HT: 18 - 36 in. BL: June - September
Flower: Corolla tubular, 2 lipped (upper lip erect, lower lip spotted and 3 lobed), lavender to rose purple, 3/4 - 1 in long, borne in showy 4 - 6 in. long terminal spikes, sometimes in leaf axils.
Leaves: Narrow, lanceolate, 3 - 5 in. long, opposite, sharply toothed.
Habitat: Open woods, fields, meadows.
Culture: Moist, well-drained soil rich in humus. Full sun to light shade.
Propagation: Seeds. Stoloniferous. Divide in spring or fall.
Note: The blooms can be moved gently around the stem and will stay in position thus giving the plant one of its common names.

269 *Prunella vulgaris* Page 186
Heal-all, Self-heal
LS: Perennial HT: 3 - 12 in. BL: May - October
Flower: Lavender to violet (occasionally white), 2 lipped (upper lip arched and hood like, lower lip 3 lobed), crowded in rounded, overlapping bracts in dense cylindrical terminal spikes (elongate after flowering).
Leaves: Ovate to lanceshaped, toothed, opposite, stems square.
Habitat: Fields, open woods, waste places, roadsides.
Culture: Shade, moisture. Creeping habit. Tends to be aggressive.
Propagation: Seed. Division.
Note: An escape from Eurasia.

42 *Pycnanthemum incanum* Page 129
Mountain mint, White horse mint
LS: Perennial HT: 3 - 6 ft. BL: June - September
Flower: Corolla small, 2 lipped, 1/4 - 3/8 in. long, white to lavender spotted purple, conspicuous bracts, borne in dense terminal and axillary clusters up to 1 in. across.

Leaves: Opposite, dark green, lanceolate to ovate, serrated margins, 1 - 4 in. long, stalked, aromatic, upper sides of leaves and bracts just below flowers covered with whitish curly hairs, basal foliage during winter.
Habitat: Woodlands, thickets, fields, roadsides.
Culture: Average garden soil, light shade, water during dry spells.
Propagation: Seed, cuttings, division every two years. Easy to naturalize but can be invasive.

225 *Salvia coccinea* Page 175
Scarlet sage
LS: Perennial HT: 1 - 2 ft. BL: May - September
Flower: Bright red, widely spaced, arranged in 3 to 9 whorls along upper part of stem. Tubular calyx surrounds tubular 2-lipped corolla (upper lip 2 lobed, lower lip 3 lobed, center one notched).
Leaves: Heart-shaped, ovate or triangular, opposite, scalloped, 1 - 2 in. square stem, dark green, hairy. Heart-shaped or triangular bracts below bloom.
Habitat: Open or thin woods, fields, roadsides.
Culture: Full sun, dry sandy soil, well drained. Tender perennial. May be grown as an annual in colder areas.
Propagation: Seed—lightly cover and keep moist. Self seeding. Stem cuttings taken in the spring.
Note: Attracts hummingbirds.

270 *Scutellaria elliptica* Page 186
Hairy skullcap
LS: Perennial HT: 12 - 18 in. BL: May - July
Flower: Blue to violet, 2 lipped, upper lip arched or hooded, lower lip striped, borne in leaf or bract axils and terminally, forming slender l-sided raceme.
Leaves: Crenate (scalloped), opposite, ovate, hairy, 1 1/2 - 2 in. long, stems square.
Habitat: Deciduous woods, slopes, clearings.
Culture: Ordinary soil.
Propagation: Seed. Division of rhizomes.
Note: Probably the most common woodland *Scutellaria*, especially in the Piedmont. There are several other species, some with showier flowers.

271 *Scutellaria montana* Page 186
Large-flowered skullcap
LS: Perennial HT: 12 - 18 in. BL: May - June
Flower: Pink to lavender, upper petal (lip) hooded and 3-lobed, lower petal unlobed, terminal.
Leaves: Opposite, ovate, wedge-shaped at base, hairy, toothed. Upper leaves crenate-serrate, square stem.
Habitat: Mixed deciduous woods with scattered pines.
Culture: Rich humus-filled soil.
Propagation: Seed. Division in March - April.
Note: Threatened species, found only in Northwest Georgia and adjacent Tennessee.

Mistletoe Family (*Loranthaceae*)

Parasitic on deciduous or evergreen trees. Yellow flowers. Leaves small, yellow-green. Waxy white poisonous berries.

43 *Phoradendron serotinum* (formerly *Phoradendron flavescens*) Page 129
Mistletoe
LS: Parasite HT: 1 ft. BL: September - October
Flower: Inconspicuous sepals, no petals, solitary or in clusters. Fruit is a clear, waxy, white small berry that appears in December.
Leaves: Small, rounded, yellow-green, thick, opposite, less than 1 in. Evergreen. Stems smooth, green.
Habitat: Deciduous trees exposed to sun.
Culture: Parasite (feeds by suckers attached to host tree).
Propagation: Usually not cultivated (parasitic); sticky seeds are spread from tree to tree by birds.
Note: Poisonous.

Mustard Family (*Cruciferae*)

Non-woody annual or perennial herbaceous plants. Flowers have 4 petals that form a cross, 4 sepals, 6 stamens, borne in racemes. Leaves simple or lobed, alternate.

44 *Dentaria diphylla* (sometimes placed in genus *Cardamine*) Page 129
Toothwort, Pepper root, Crinkleroot
LS: Perennial HT: 5 - 10 in. BL: April
Flower: White, fading pink, 4 petals, cross-shaped, 4 sepals (fall early), 3/4 in. long, borne in loose terminal clusters.
Leaves: Basal—3-lobed, serrated; long-stalked, usually evergreen, nearly opposite, located just below bloom.
Habitat: Wooded slopes, along streams, moist woods.
Culture: Rich moist soil, shade.
Propagation: Seed sown as soon as collected. Divide and transplant while dormant. Rhizomes break easily. Rhizomes run along soil surface just below leaf mold.

189 *Hesperis matronalis* Page 166
Dame's rocket
LS: Perennial HT: 2 - 3 ft. BL: May - August
Flower: Lilac, pink or white, small yellow eye, 4-petaled, calyx tubular, borne in loose terminal panicles. Fragrant, accentuated at night.
Leaves: Oblong, toothed, alternate.
Habitat: Fields, roadsides.
Culture: Sun or part shade, rich moist soil.
Propagation: Seed (need light to germinate). Flowers 2nd year.
Note: An escape, one of the more commonly used European wildflowers.

Nightshade Family (*Solanaceae*)

Mostly annual or perennial herbs with a few shrubs and trees. Leaves vary in size and shape, entire or variously dissected, usually alternate. Corolla usually a flat tube, flower parts mostly in fives; white, yellow or purple. Fruit a pod or berry with many seeds. Some species poisonous but also includes tomatoes, potatoes, peppers, etc.

142 *Physalis heterophylla* Page 154

Clammy ground cherry, Husk tomato

LS: Perennial HT: 1 - 2 ft. BL: May - November

Flower: Yellow, dark eye or center, pendulant, bell-shaped, hang singly from leaf axils.

Leaves: Upper leaves often opposite, lower leaves alternate, ovate, to 3 in. long, cordate, coarse, hairy.

Habitat: Thin open woods, waste places.

Culture: Dry sandy soil, sun.

Propagation: Seed, soft cuttings, division.

Orchid Family (*Orchidaceae*)

Terrestrial or epiphyte herbs. Flowers irregular, 3 green or colored sepals, 2 lateral petals, 3rd petal usually larger sometimes saclike or forming a lip, usually only 1 fertile stamen; highly modified inferior ovary. Very small seeds. Leaves entire, parallel-veined. Grow from rhizome or fleshy rootstock.

45, *Cypripedium acaule* Pages 130, 166

190 Pink lady's slipper, Moccasin flower

LS: Perennial HT: 6 - 15 in. BL: April - May

Flower: Solitary, 2 - 3 in., pink, occasionally white, veiny lip petal an inflated pouch, sepals and petals greenish brown and spreading.

Leaves: Two, large, oval and basal, dark green above, silvery and hairy beneath, deciduous. Stem leafless, rising directly from ground.

Habitat: Partial shade under pines.

Culture: Soil very acid, humus filled, well drained. Temperamental but will thrive if properly cared for and given the right conditions. Dependent upon fungi that exist in its natural setting.

Propagation: Division of clumps. Leave one bud to each plant. Set bud just beneath soil surface. Roots should be no more than 2 - 3 in. deep. Transplant in early fall or spring when plants are dormant.

Note: Threatened species in Georgia. Considered unusually showy and worthy of protection. Name derived from unusual pouch shape of lower petal which resembles a lady's slipper or moccasin. Generic name Greek *cyris* means Venus and *pedilon* means slipper.

143 *Cypripedium calceolus* var. *pubescen* (large) Page 154
144 *Cypripedium calceolus* var. *parviflorum* (small) Page 154
Yellow lady's slipper
LS: Perennial HT: 8 - 22 in. BL: April - May
Flower: Yellow inflated, saclike lip, 1 - 2 in., 1 to 3 terminal flowers, long wavy brownish sepals, fragrant.
Leaves: Leafy stalk, leaves broadly ovate with pronounced parallel veins, 3 to 5, alternately arranged on stem, green above and beneath.
Habitat: Under deciduous trees (maples, birches, oaks, etc.).
Culture: Rich, woodsy soil, slightly acid to neutral.
Propagation: Division of clumps. Leave one bud to each plant. Set bud just beneath the surface of the soil. Transplant in fall or early spring when plants dormant. Roots should be no more than 2 - 3 in. deep.
Note: Threatened species in Georgia. Considered unusually showy and worthy of protection.

46 *Goodyera pubescens* Page 130
Rattlesnake orchid, Downy rattlesnake plantain, Latticeleaf
LS: Perennial HT: 6 - 16 in. BL: June - July
Flower: Small, about 1/4 in. long, white or tinged with green, upper sepal joins at edges of two lateral petals to form a hood over a pouch-like lip, side sepals ovate, borne in a dense terminal spikelike raceme up to 5 in. long.
Leaves: 1 - 3 in. long, up to 1 in. wide, oblong to ovate, 3 to 8 form a basal rosetts, conspicuous checkered leaf pattern (white veins and cross veins on a dark blue-green background), evergreen. Leafless woolly stem with scalelike bracts.
Habitat: Coniferous and deciduous woods, well-drained wooded slopes.
Culture: Rich, woodsy soil, dry or moist, shade.
Propagation: Division.

171 *Platanthera ciliaris* (also known as *Habenaria ciliaris*) Page 161
Yellow fringed orchid, Orange plume
LS: Perennial HT: 1 - 2 1/2 ft. BL: June - August
Flower: Small, with fringed lip, yellow or orange, form an elongated, showy terminal raceme.
Leaves: Lanceolate, sheathing the stem, upper leaves smaller (pointed bracts).
Habitat: Bogs, moist woods, wet meadows, slopes.
Culture: Acid soil, shade, peaty.
Propagation: Transplants fairly easy. Let divide naturally. Seed are very fine.
Note: Many nurseries sell terrestrial native orchids but rarely are the plants propagated. Usually *Habenaria*-type orchids are short-lived in gardens and are, therefore, unsuitable. Because some types are extremely rare they should not be promoted as garden subjects. They are best observed and studied in nature preserves. They should be moved from their native habitat only when in danger of being destroyed.

302 *Malaxis unifolia* Page 194
Adder's mouth (green)
LS: Perennial HT: 4 - 8 in. BL: June - August
Flower: Tiny, green, lateral petals threadlike, elongated cluster on solitary stem.
Leaves: Single, bright green, oval, pointed, clasping.

Habitat: Woods, thickets.
Culture: Rich, humus-filled soil, dry to moist, acid.
Propagation: Division.

191 *Orchis spectabilis* (sometimes known as *Galearis spectabilis*) Page 166
Showy orchis
LS: Perennial HT: 6 - 8 in. BL: April - May
Flower: White spurred lower lip, pink to lavender hood, about 1 in. long, a terminal spike of from 3 - 12 blooms emerge from axils or bracts. Fragrant.
Leaves: Two, large, basal, thick, glossy, green, oval, sheathing the stem. Bracts just below the flower. Deciduous.
Habitat: Mixed woods, moist slopes.
Culture: Moist, rich woods, loamy soil, acid, partial shade.
Propagation: Transplant easily. Divide rootstalk when dormant. Seeds very powdery. Catch in plastic bag. Hard to propagate.

47 *Spiranthes cernua* Page 130
Autumn ladies tresses, Nodding ladies tresses
LS: Perennial HT: 6 - 24 in. BL: August - September
Flower: White to cream, about 1/2 in. long, united side and upper petals form a hood over lower wavy petal or lip, fragrant, nod or arch slightly downward, spiral in rows around stem to form a dense slender spike.
Leaves: Stem leaves narrow and grasslike, resemble bracts and hug the stem, basal leaves linear.
Habitat: Roadsides, wet meadows and fields.
Culture: Wet soil, partial to full sun.
Propagation: Seed, transplant easily.

48 *Spiranthes gracilis* (also known as *Spiranthes lacera* var. *gracilis*) Page 130
Slender ladies' tresses
LS: Perennial HT: 6 - 18 in. BL: August - October
Flower: Dainty, tiny and irregular with 1 sepal and 2 petals forming a hood, third petal forms a lip, usually white with a central green stripe. Flowers arranged in a single closely packed spiral around the slender stem.
Leaves: Basal and lanceolate. Wither by flowering time.
Habitat: Dry fields, open woods, hillsides.
Culture: Slightly acid soil.
Propagation: Flower from seed in 3 years. Move tuberous, fleshy roots and divide in winter.

Parsley or Carrot Family (*Umbelliferae*)

Herbaceous annual, biennial or perennial plants. Flowers numerous, small, 5 sepals, 5 petals and 5 stamens, borne in compound umbels or flat-topped clusters. Leaves finely cut, alternate or basal, compound.

49 *Daucus carota* Page 131

Queen Anne's lace, Bird's nest

LS: Biennial HT: 1 - 4 ft. BL: May - September

Flower: Clusters of small, lacy, white flowers arranged in 2 - 4 in. wide heads, 1 deep purple floret at center of umbel. Slightly rounded. Erect, usually branched.

Leaves: Finely divided, feathery or fernlike, alternately arranged on a hairy stem.

Habitat: Dry fields, road sides, waste places.

Propagation: Seed sown in the fall. Strong, long taproot makes transplanting difficult.

Note: An escape from Eurasia-widely naturalized. Bloom said to resemble Queen Anne's lace head dress. When bloom fades the head becomes concave and resembles a small bird's nest.

Pea Family (*Leguminosae*)

Very large family of trees, shrubs, herbs or vines. Flowers usually irregular, 5 petals (2 lower ones keeled, 2 side ones winged, upper one a banner), 10 stamens, superior ovary. Leaves usually alternate, compound with stipules, tendrils or thorns. Roots contain nitrogen-fixing bacteria.

50 *Baptisia pendula* Page 131

White wild indigo

LS: Perennial HT: 1 - 2 ft. BL: April - May

Flower: White or cream, 5 petals (pea-like), 1/2 - 1 in. across, borne in loose terminal racemes, 4 - 6 in. long, showy.

Leaves: Oblong, 1 1/2 - 2 in. long, palmately divided into 3 leaflets, gray-green, alternate.

Habitat: Open woods, pinelands, edges of woods and fields.

Culture: Average to rich loose soil, good drainage, full to partial sun.

Propagation: Seeds (soak overnight), need warmth for germination. Division. Transplant seedlings.

145 *Baptisia tinctoria* Page 155

Wild indigo, False indigo, Yellow indigo

LS: Perennial HT: 1 - 2 ft. BL: June - September

Flower: Golden yellow, 5 lobes, upper two united into large lobe (pea like), 1/2 - 1 in. long, in numerous but few-flowered loose terminal racemes.

Leaves: Blue-green, petioled, alternate, palmately compound, 3 small leaflets, ovate (clover-like), much branched, bushy growth habit.

Habitat: Meadows, open deciduous woodlands.

Culture: Dry, porous sandy soil, full sun, slightly acid.

Propagation: Plant ripe seed in open ground in fall or spring.

272 *Lupinus perennis* Page 186

Wild lupine, Quaker bonnets

LS: Perennial HT: 8 - 20 in. BL: April - July

Flower: Blue, varying to pink or white, pea-like (calyx 2 - lipped, standard obicular, 2 wings obovate), up to 2/3 in. long, many forming upright elongated terminal raceme.

Leaves: Deciduous, palmately compound (7 - 11 leaflets), sessile, lanceolate up to 2 in. long, hairy, alternate.

Lupinus villosus
Lady lupine
LS: Perennial HT: 1 - 2 ft. BL: April - July
Flower: Purple to reddish or lavender with deeper shade spot, pea-like (similar to *L. perennis*), many form dense upright terminal raceme.
Leaves: Evergreen, simple (with only one leaflet).
Habitat (both species): Thin woods, dry open woods, fields, clearings, sandhills.
Culture: Dry sandy soil, good drainage, sun, neutral soil.
Propagation: Seed sown in early spring. Seeds very hard. Scarify overnight. Self seeding. Division in early spring. Deep taproot makes difficult to transplant. Allow plenty of space in the garden.

Phlox Family (*Polemoniaceae*)

Perennial or annual herbs, some shrubs and small trees. Phlox has 5 flat petals joined at narrow corolla tube (concealing 5 stamens and style). Leaves simple or compound. *Polemonium* flowers are bell shaped with 5 joined petals, 5 stamens, 3-pronged style. Leaves pinnately divided or simple, usually opposite, entire.

226 *Ipomosis rubra* Page 175
Standing cypress, Scarlet gilia, Spanish lockspur, Texas plume
LS: Biennial HT: 2 - 6 ft. BL: May - September
Flower: Bright red corolla, inside yellow dotted with red, tubular with five flaring lobes, up to 1 in. long, borne in a long, narrow unbranched inflorescence.
Leaves: Pinnately divided into very narrow hairlike segments, about 1 in. long, numerous.
Habitat: Open, sandy places.
Culture: Sandy soil, full to partial sun, good drainage.
Propagation: Seeds.

273 *Phlox divaricata* Page 187
Blue phlox, Wild sweet William
LS: Perennial HT: 9 - 18 in. BL: April - July
Flower: Light blue, tubular with 5 spreading lobes, loose spreading cluster.
Leaves: Opposite, oblong.
Habitat: Rich, open woods.
Culture: Moist, humus rich acid to neutral soil.
Propagation: Division in spring after flowering. Seed. Self seeding.

192 *Phlox drummondii* Page 166
Summer phlox
LS: Annual HT: 8 - 16 in. BL: April - July
Flower: White, pink, magenta, tubular with 5 spreading lobes, 1 in. wide, dark eye, borne in tight clusters.
Leaves: Lanceolate, 1 - 3 in., sticky, stem branched at top.
Habitat: Roadsides, waste places, fields.
Culture: Moist, humus rich acid to neutral soil.
Propagation: Seed.

193 *Phlox subulata* Page 167
Moss phlox, Moss pink, Thrift
LS: Perennial HT: 2 - 6 in. BL: April - July
Flower: Pink, purple or white in terminal clusters on stem ends, 3/4 in., tubular with 5 spreading lobes.
Leaves: Closely set, needle like, to 1 in. long, opposite, evergreen, extensively branched, forms dense mats.
Habitat: Fields, roadsides, rocky hills, open woods, meadows.
Culture: Moist, humus rich, acid to neutral soil, filtered sun.
Propagation: Division in spring after flowering. Self seeding.
Note: Widely used. Native to Middle Atlantic states. Many native phloxes are difficult to identify.

Pink Family (*Caryophyllaceae*)

Temperate herbaceous plants, annual or perennial, deciduous. Flowers 4 - 5 petals usually notched, 5 sepals, 8 - 10 stamens, solitary or borne in a cyme. Leaves opposite or whorled, mostly narrow, simple, entire. Swollen joints or nodes.

194 *Dianthus armeria* Page 167
Deptford pink
LS: Perennial HT: 6 - 20 in. BL: May - September
Flower: Deep pink with white spots, 5 jagged petals, 1/2 in. wide.
Leaves: Long and narrow, erect, 1/4 in. long, opposite, hairy. Lance-shaped bracts below flowers.
Habitat: Dry fields, roadsides, pastures.
Culture: Ordinary soil, sun.
Propagation: Seed, division, cuttings.
Note: An escape from central Europe but widely naturalized in Georgia.

195 *Dianthus deltoides* Page 167
Maiden pink
LS: Perennial HT: 5 - 9 in. BL: May - June
Flower: Deep rose pink, 5 rounded, much-toothed petals wtih dark circle or "eye" at base, solitary, 1/2 in. wide, tubed calyx.
Leaves: Opposite, linear, up to 1 in. long, gray-green, erect stems.
Habitat: Dry fields, roadsides.
Culture: Ordinary soil, well drained, alkaline.
Propagation: Seed. Stem cuttings. Division.
Note: An escape from Europe.

51 *Lychnis alba* (alternatively *Silene alba*) Page 131
Evening lychnis, White campion
LS: Biennial or short-lived perennial HT: 1 - 2 ft. BL: May - September
Flower: White, sometimes pale pink, 5 deeply notched petals, 5 curved styles, tubular

inflated sticky calyx, 20 purplish veins, toothed, 1 in. wide. Male and female flowers on separate plants. Male has fewer veins on calyx. Evening or night flowering. Very fragrant.
Leaves: Opposite, hairy, ovate to lanceolate, stalkless, 1 1/2 - 4 in. long. Much branched hairy stem. Sprawling habit.
Habitat: Fields, roadsides, waste places.
Culture: Ordinary soil, sun.
Propagation: Seed. Division, stem cuttings.
Note: An escape from North Africa and Eurasia.

196 *Lychnis coronaria* Page 167
Rose campion, Mullein pink, Dusty miller
LS: Perennial HT: 12 - 24 in. BL: May - August
Flower: Deep rose or magenta, 5 flaring petals, to 1 in. across, notched, solitary.
Leaves: Opposite, densely woolly, blue-green to whitish, oval, branching.
Habitat: Roadsides, dry open woods.
Culture: Sun or partial shade, clay or loam.
Propagation: Seed or division. Self seeding. Forms dense mats.
Note: An escape from North Africa and Eurasia.

197 *Saponaria officinalis* Page 168
Bouncing Bet, Soapwort
LS: Perennial HT: 1 - 2 ft. BL: May - September
Flower: Pink or white, delicate, 1 in. across, 5 long petals appearing scalloped or notched on tips, reflexed slightly. Form dense terminal clusters. Borne from upper leaf axils. Fragrant. Sometimes double. Bracts just below bloom.
Leaves: Opposite, lanceolate, 2 - 3 in. long, conspicuously ribbed. Lower leaves almost whorled. Deciduous. Stout stems appear swollen at joints or nodes.
Habitat: Roadsides, open fields, fencerows, railroad banks.
Culture: Ordinary garden soil.
Propagation: Seed. Division of rootstock in spring or fall. Spreads by underground runners. Tends to be aggressive, forming large colonies.
Note: An escape from Eurasia. Roots used to produce a soapy lather.

Silene armeria
Catchfly, None so pretty
LS: Annual or biennial HT: 1 - 2 ft. BL: July - September
Flower: Pink or white, clustered at top of branches, calyx tubular, 5 petals, 1/2 in. across.
Leaves: Opposite, untoothed, lance shaped, sticky.
Habitat: Dry, open rocky woods, fields.
Culture: Ordinary garden soil.
Propagation: By seed sown in fall or spring.

Silene carolinana
Wild pink
LS: Perennial HT: 5 - 10 in. BL: May
Flower: Bright pink or white to light pink, clustered, 5 petals, 3/4 in. wide, calyx tubular, borne in sparse flat terminal clusters.
Leaves: Narrow, wedge to lance shaped, opposite, upper stem sticky, unbranched.

Habitat: Dry, open rocky woods, fields, sandhills.
Culture: Ordinary garden soil.
Propagation: Seed or division.

198 *Silene polypetela* Page 168
Fringed campion
LS: Perennial HT: 8 - 20 in. BL: April - May
Flower: Five separate petals, pink, deeply dissected on tips, borne terminally and in upper leaf axils, feathery in appearance.
Leaves: Spatulate, opposite, hairy, most stems decumbent.
Habitat: Rich, deciduous woods, hillsides.
Culture: Rich, woodsy soil.
Propagation: Division. Stems are decumbent and will root.
Note: Endangered species; thrives on soils with little leaf litter; extremely delicate in wild where they rarely form viable seed. New to horticulture; tricky to establish but extremely showy.

227 *Silene virginica* Page 175
Fire pink
LS: Perennial* HT: 1 - 2 ft. BL: April - July
Flower: Bright red, about 1 in. in diameter, with 5 deeply notched narrow petals. Borne in loose clusters on weak and hairy stems.
Leaves: Basal rosette, semi-evergreen with 2 - 4 pairs cauline leaves, opposite and unstalked.
Habitat: Open woods, rocky slopes, roadsides.
Culture: Acid soil, dry, sandy or rocky, well-drained, full to partial sun.
Propagation: By seed. Bloom 2nd year. Transplant when dormant.

*Short-lived.

Pipewort Family (*Eriocaulaceae*)

Perennial and sometimes annual herbs (may be aquatic or soil grown). Flowers have involucrate heads, small. Leaves rushlike in basal rosettes.

Eriocaulon decangulare
Pipewort, Hatpins, Buttonrods
LS: Perennial HT: 3 - 6 in. BL: July - September
Flower: Small, 1/2 in., dense gray or white woolly heads, borne on tip of slender leafless stalk, 2 petals, bracts between and beneath petals.
Leaves: Basal, linear, rushlike.
Habitat: Wet pine woodlands, cypress swamps, ditches, bogs.
Culture: Sandy or peaty moist soil, still water.
Propagation: Division.

Pitcher Plant Family (*Sarraceniaceae*)

Bog herbs, insectivorous, growing from rhizomes. Flowers nodding, 5 broad petals, 5 broad sepals, numerous stamens. Leaves tubular, basal.

Sarracenia
Pitcher plant
LS: Perennial HT: 1 - 2 ft. BL: March - May
Flower: Single, nodding, 5 sepals, 5 petals (form inverted umbrella), many stamens, color range from yellow to purple
Leaves: Basal, shaped like "pitchers," tubes or trumpets. Insectivorous.
Habitat: (all species) Swamps, bogs, wet places.
Culture: (all species) Acid bogs, sphagnum, sandy peat. Keep crowns near surface of water. Sun.
Propagation: Seed prolifically. Sow as soon as ripe. Flowering takes 3 - 5 years. Division of crowns or rootstock in March or April.

146 *Sarracenia flava* Page 155
Golden trumpets
Flower: Single, nodding, yellow, 2 - 4 in. wide, 5 oblong, curving petals, musty odor.
Leaves: Erect, trumpet shaped, yellow-green with red or purple veins on throat. "Lid" over hollow opening.

Sarracenia leucophylla
White-topped pitcher plant, White trumpet
Flower: Nodding, red-purple.
Leaves: Erect, upper portion white-spotted, sometimes veined purple.

147 *Sarracenia minor* Page 155
Hooded pitcher plant
Flower: Sepals and petals yellow.
Leaves: Hollow, opening arched by a hood, green translucent blotch, veined purple.

Sarracenia psittacina
Parrot pitcher plant
Flower: Red-orange, borne on a single stem, petals rolled.
Leaves: Basal rosette, evergreen. Hood incurved, marked with red or purple.
Note: *S. flava, S. leucophylla, S. minor* and *S. psittacina*, along with *S. purpurea* and *S. rubra*, have been exploited and are threatened with habitat loss. The first four are on the threatened species list while the last two are endangered species in Georgia.

Poppy Family (*Papaveraceae*)

Herbaceous annuals or perennials, some shrubs. Showy flowers, 4 - 12 petals, 2 - 3 sepals (fall before flower opens), numerous stamens. Leaves lobed or cut. Exudes milky juice.

52 *Sanguinaria canadensis* Page 131

Bloodroot

LS: Perennial HT: 6 - 12 in. BL: March - May

Flower: Large, pure white, star shaped, 8 - 12 petals, yellow center, solitary, 1 1/2 - 2 in. wide, closing at night. Short lived.

Leaves: Large, leathery, wrapped around flower bud as it emerges. Unfolds after flower withers. Palmate, veined. Deciduous.

Habitat: Rich deciduous woods, low hillsides, along streams.

Culture: Humus rich soil, semi-shade, moist, moderately acid.

Propagation: Seeds sown as soon as ripe. Self seeding. Bloom in 2 - 3 years. Divide rhizomes in fall.

Note: One of the showiest early spring wildflowers-found in all parts of Georgia except for coastal areas.

148 *Stylophorum diphyllum* Page 155

Celadine poppy, Wood poppy

LS: Perennial HT: 10 - 16 in. BL: March - May

Flower: Four fragile rounded petals, 2 hairy sepals, numerous stamens, 1 - 1 1/2 in. wide, yellow, solitary.

Leaves: Two, opposite, large, pale, deeply lobed, just below inflorescence, whitish bloom underneath. Other leaves basal, lobed.

Habitat: Damp woods, bluffs.

Culture: Rich moist soil, semi-shade.

Propagation: Seed, stem cuttings, division.

Note: A rare plant in Georgia, known only from the Cumberland Plateau, but easily grown in gardens where it soon develops a mind of its own.

Primrose Family (*Primulaceae*)

Perennial or annual herbs growing from rhizomes or tubers. Flowers usually 5 petals, each stamen at center of a petal (instead of between), sometimes on leafless stalk. Leaves simple, undivided, opposite, whorled or basal.

Anagallis arvensis

Scarlet pimpernel, Poor man's weatherglass

LS: Annual HT: 4 - 12 in. BL: June - August

Flower: Small, 1/4 in. wide, starlike with 5-lobed corolla, bright red or orange, many stamens, borne on long nodding stalks growing singly from leaf axils, petals toothed, open in morning on sunny days, close before a storm.

Leaves: Ovate, opposite, 1/2 - 1 in. long, sessile.

Habitat: Waste places, roadsides.

Culture: Sandy soil.

Propagation: Seed.

Note: An escape from Europe.

53 *Dodecatheon meadia* Page 132

Shooting star

LS: Perennial HT: 8 - 15 in. BL: March - May

Flower: White, sometimes pink, about 1 in. long, 5 petals project backward, joined stamens, nodding in a terminal umbel, leafless flowering stalk.

Leaves: Basal rosette, lanceolate, 6 in. long, green. Deciduous.

Habitat: Rich, open deciduous woods, meadows, prairies.

Culture: Slightly alkaline to neutral soil, shade or partial shade, moist soil rich in humus, good drainage.

Propagation: Division of rootstock in fall, retaining bud for each section.

149 *Lysimachia ciliata* (alternatively *Steironema ciliatum*) Page 156

Fringed loosestrife

LS: Perennial HT: 12 - 18 in. BL: June - August

Flower: Small, 3/4 in., yellow, 5 petals with sharp points (star-like), grow from leaf axils, nodding.

Leaves: Opposite, lanceolate, 2 - 3 in. petioles, hairy.

150 *Lysimachia quadrifolia* Page 156

Whorled loosestrife

LS: Perennial HT: 1 - 2 ft. BL: June - August

Flower: Small, 1/2 in., 5 petals, yellow-reddish around center, from leaf whorls.

Leaves: Whorled (usually 4) 1 - 3 in., light green, lanceolate.

Habitat: (both species) Dry or moist open woods, thickets and fields.

Culture: (both species) Ordinary garden soil.

Propagation: (both species) Division. Self seeding.

Purslane Family (*Portulacaceae*)

Annual or perennial succulent shrubs and herbs. Flowers usually regular with 5 petals, 2 sepals, 4 - 5 stamens. Short lived. Leaves usually opposite, toothless, simple, entire, fleshy. Often prostrate habit.

199 *Claytonia virginica* Page 168

Narrowleaf spring beauty

LS: Perennial HT: 3 - 6 in. BL: March - May

Flower: Five ray florets, to 1/2 in. wide, white to pale pink, veined dark pink, borne in loose terminal clusters, very dainty and graceful. Close at night.

Leaves: Two, narrow and long, grasslike, opposite, midway up stem.

Habitat: Wooded slopes, moist deciduous woods.

Culture: Rich, humusy woods soil, damp, partial shade, neutral to slightly acid soil.

Propagation: Seed. Self seeding.

Portulaca pilosa

Hairy portulaca, Rose moss

LS: Annual HT: 2 - 8 in. BL: June - October

Flower: Five petals, magenta, 1/2 in. wide, many stamens, open for 1 day.

Leaves: Linear to spatulate, succulent like, branching; on stems with tufts of white shaggy hairs.
Habitat: Thin scrub, open fields.
Culture: Dry sandy soil, full sun.
Propagation: Seed.

Rose Family (*Rosaceae*)

Woody and herbaceous herbs (usually perennial), shrubs or trees (deciduous and evergreen). Flowers have 5 rounded petals, 5 sepals, united at base, numerous stamens, ovary nearly inferior. Leaves alternate, with stipules, simple or compound.

54 *Aruncus dioicus* Page 132
Goat's beard
LS: Perennial HT: 3 - 5 ft. BL: May - June
Flower: Very small, creamy white, 5 petals, in showy and feathery panicles (3 - 5 in. wide, 6 - 10 in. long). Male and female flowers on different plants.
Leaves: Large, feathery, alternately compound, leaflets oval and pointed, 1 1/2 in. long.
Habitat: Deciduous, rich woods, ravines, woodland clearings.
Culture: Partial shade, rich moist soil.
Propagation: Seed or division (in spring or early fall).

151 *Potentilla canadensis* Page 156
Dwarf cinquefoil, Five fingers
LS: Perennial HT: 2 - 6 in. BL: March - June
Flower: Yellow, solitary, to 3/4 in. wide, 5 petals, 5 sepal-like bracts, numerous pistils, first flower grows from axil of first stem leaf.
Leaves: Compound, palmate, stemmed, usually 5 oblong leaflets each 1 1/2 in. long, toothed above middle, rounded. Silvery downy stems, creeping habit (spread by slender runners).
Habitat: Open places, roadsides, fields.
Culture: Dry, well-drained, ordinary garden soil, sun.
Propagation: Seed. Prostrate stems root at nodes. Divide rootstock.

Potentilla simplex
Common cinquefoil
LS: Perennial HT: 6 - 12 in. BL: March - June
Flower: Similar to *P. canadensis* except first flower arises from the axil of second stem leaf. Resemble wild strawberry.
Leaves: Similar to *P. canadensis* but larger leaflets. Stems more erect (arch and root at the tip).
Habitat: Same.
Culture: Same.
Propagation: Same.

Saxifrage Family (*Saxifragaceae*)

Mostly perennial shrubs and herbs. Flowers are small, 4-5 petals (often jointed), 5-10 stamens, borne in loose clusters. Leaves usually basal forming a rosette. Stem leaves alternate or opposite, simple or compound.

55 *Astilbe biternata* Page 132

False goat's beard

LS: Perennial HT: 2 - 5 ft. BL: May - July

Flower: Yellowish-white, small and numerous, borne in profuse elongated feathery terminal clusters.

Leaves: Large, to 2 in. wide, bright green, finely cut, compound, divided into 3 segments which are divided into 3-lobed or toothed leaflets, terminal leaflet 3-lobed. Deciduous. Stalk hairy.

Habitat: Open woods, along edges of woods.

Culture: Shade or part shade, rich moist soil.

Propagation: Seed or division.

Heuchera americana

American alumroot

LS: Perennial HT: 8 - 20 in. BL: May - June

Flower: Very small, 1/4 in., greenish or purplish, bell-shaped, prominent stamen, forming long, loose and narrow terminal panicle.

Leaves: Basal, long stalked, sharply lobed (shaped similar to maple leaf), 3 - 4 in. wide, hairy, evergreen.

Habitat: Cliffs, ledges, woods, slopes, rocky ground.

Culture: Acid to neutral soil, shade or partial shade, loam.

Propagation: Seed or division.

56 *Mitella diphylla* Page 132

Miterwort, Bishop's cap

LS: Perennial HT: 8 - 15 in. BL: April - June

Flower: Inconspicuous, creamy white, shaped like tiny fringed bells, delicate, spaced singly along upper portion of stem, forming slender raceme. Several flowering stems may emerge from a root.

Leaves: Heart-shaped, 3 to 5 lobes, basal, to 3 in. long, stalked. Pair of stemless small leaves, opposite and clasping on flower stem below raceme.

Habitat: Stream banks, deciduous wooded slopes, rocky woods.

Culture: Rich woodsy soil with plenty of leaf mold, shade.

Propagation: Seed or division.

57 *Tiarella cordifolia* Page 133

Foamflower, False-miterwort

LS: Perennial HT: 8 - 12 in. BL: April - May

Flower: Small, delicate, 5-petaled, white, in feathery elongated single terminal raceme or loose cluster, 4 - 6 in. long.

Leaves: Green basal leaves, long petioled, slightly hairy, heart-shaped, sharply lobed and toothed margins, 2 - 4 in. long. Stem generally leafless, grown directly from base of plant

Habitat: Moist deciduous woodland, woody slopes.
Culture: Partial shade, rich soil with plenty of leaf mold, slightly acid to neutral. Easy to grow.
Propagation: Seeds sown in the fall. Divide rhizomes. Spreads by underground stems. Transplant runners on young plants after flowering.
Note: Some variants of this species produce stolons; there are also many cultivars with unique foliage coloration. All in all one of the favorite native American wildflowers for rocky areas or borders.

Sedge Family (*Cyperaceae*)

Perennial herbs of wet spots. Inflorescence has 1 or more small spikes which emerge from bract axils. Leaves grass or rush like, sheathed at base. Stem 3-sided.

Dichromena colorata
White-topped sedge, Star rush
LS: Perennial HT: 1 - 2 ft. BL: March - November
Flower: Minute, enclosed in oblong white scales in small spikes, forming a tight cluster, 2/3 in. wide, borne on tip of stem. Enclosed at base by long, drooping white and wide spreading bracts with narrow green tips (usually less than 7). Showy.
Leaves: Grasslike, long and narrow. Stem triangular, leafless, unbranched.
Habitat: Swamps, marshes, bogs, thin woods.
Culture: Wet soil.
Propagation: Seeds sown in the fall. Division of clumps.

Dichromena latifolia (Broadleaf white-topped sedge) is similar to *D. colorata* but is showier and has 7 - 10 bracts.

Snapdragon or Foxglove Family (*Scrophulariaceae*)

Herbs (some semi-parasitic) and shrubs. Flowers have swollen corolla tubes that flare and two lips (2-lobed upper lip and 3-lobed lower lip) which may sometimes be more regular, usually 4 stamens. Leaves simple.

274 *Agalinis purpurea* (also known as *Gerardia purpurea*) Page 187
Gerardia, Purple false foxglove, Autumn bells
LS: Annual HT: 8 - 24 in. BL: July - September
Flower: Rose-pink to purple, bell-shaped, 5 fused sepals, spreading and unequal, lobes shorter than tube, to 1 in. wide, bloom in leaf axils.
Leaves: Linear, opposite, narrow, 1 - 1 1/2 in. long, branching.
Habitat: Thin woods, fields, meadows.
Culture: Damp, acid soil.
Propagation: Seed.
Note: May be semi-parasitic on grass roots.

Aureolaria laevigata (also known as *Gerardia laevigata*)
Smooth false foxglove
LS: Perennial HT: 2 - 3 ft. BL: July - September
Flower: Yellow, bell shaped, 5 lobes, 1 - 1 1/2 in. long, borne in clusters.
Leaves: Opposite, lanceolate, smooth, short petioles (almost sessile).
Habitat: Dry oak woods.
Culture: Ordinary, rich garden soil.
Propagation: Seed or division.
Note: May be semi-parasitic on roots of oak trees.

152 *Aureolaria pedicularia* (also known as *Gerardia pedicularia*) Page 156
False foxglove, Fern-leaved foxglove, Fever-flower
LS: Perennial HT: 1 - 4 ft. BL: August - September
Flower: Yellow, bell-shaped corolla, flaring into five almost equal lobes, upper two joined, 1 - 1 1/2 in. long, 1 in. wide, borne on short stalks in upper leaf axils.
Leaves: Pinnately divided with blunt teeth, 1 - 3 in. long, opposite, much branched, hairy and sticky.
Habitat: Thin oak woods, thickets.
Culture: Dry, acid soil, partial shade.
Propagation: Seed.
Note: May be semi-parasitic on roots of oak trees.

228 *Castilleja coccinea* Page 175
Indian paint brush, Painted cup
LS: Biennial HT: 6 - 18 in. BL: May - July
Flower: Light green, almost hidden, between 3-lobed showy red-orange tipped bracts, light green at base, borne in dense spikes in leaf axils.
Leaves: Basal rosette, oblong leaves, hairy, with 1 unbranched stem. True leaves cleft, greenish yellow, incised.
Habitat: Rock ledges and cliffs, fields, wet meadows, thin open deciduous woods.
Culture: Sun or light shade, moist sandy and humus filled soil. Difficult to grow. Reputed to be a partial parasite on roots of other plants or dependent for food on the roots of certain fungi.
Propagation: Seed, sown as soon as ripe. Bloom second year.

58 *Chelone glabra* Page 133
White turtlehead
LS: Perennial HT: 1 - 4 ft. BL: July - September
Flower: Off white, often lavender or pink tinged near tips, corolla irregular, 1 - 1 1/2 in. long, notched upper lip arches over hairy lower lip, borne in tight terminal clusters.
Leaves: Lanceolate or ovate, sharply toothed, opposite, 3 - 6 in. long.
Habitat: Wet thickets and meadows, streambanks, low grounds.
Culture: Light, humus-rich soil, constantly moist, sun, acid or neutral.
Propagation: Seed, cuttings, division.

200 *Chelone lyonii* Page 168
Turtlehead, Snakehead
LS: Perennial HT: 1 - 3 ft. BL: August - September
Flower: Pink or rose-pink, 1 in. long, corolla irregular, inflated, petals join to form a tube

which spreads into 2 lips; slightly notched upper lip arches over the lower lip; lower lip three-lobed, yellow woolly beard inside; borne in a tight cluster at terminal end of stem.
Leaves: Dark green, broad, ovate, petioled, coarsely toothed, opposite.
Habitat: Wet open woods and meadows, streambanks, swamps, marshes.
Culture: Humus enriched soil, moderately moist to wet, mulch to conserve moisture, partial shade.
Propagation: Seeds (stratify or sow in the fall), stem cuttings, divide in early spring or late fall while dormant (fibrous root system).
Note: *Chelone oblique* has pink to purple flowers and lanceolate, toothed leaves.

153 *Linaria vulgaris* Page 157
Butter-and-eggs, Wild snapdragon
LS: Perennial HT: 1 - 2 ft. BL: June - September
Flower: Yellow-tipped with orange on lower lip, about 1 in. long, irregular corolla has protruding spur at base. Borne in showy terminal clublike spike.
Leaves: Numerous, very narrow, pointed on both ends, gray-green, upper alternate, lower opposite.
Habitat: Roadsides, fields.
Culture: Ordinary garden soil.
Propagation: Seed (bloom second year) or division.
Note: An escape from Eurasia—naturalized rarely in North Georgia.

229 *Pedicularis canadensis* Page 176
Lousewort, Wood betony, Fernleaf
LS: Perennial HT: 5 - 10 in. BL: April - June
Flower: Corolla irregular, two-lipped, upper lip hooded, lower lip 3 lobed, spreading downward, to 3/4 in. long, bicolored (pale yellow, reddish brown, purple), borne in whorled dense terminal clusters.
Leaves: Narrow, oblong, deeply cut, fernlike, 3 - 5 in. long, alternate.
Habitat: Rich open woods, meadows.
Culture: Rich soil, well drained.
Propagation: Seed, division. May be partially parasitic.

201 *Penstemon digitalis* Page 169
Foxglove, Beardtongue
LS: Perennial HT: 2 - 4 ft. BL: May - June
Flower: Tubular, 1 - 1 1/2 in. long, unevenly 5-lobed, 2 lipped (2 lobes in upper lip are erect, 3 lobes in lower lip project outward), pink or white (may be violet tinged), flower cluster stalked, borne in pairs from upper leaf axils, 5 stamens, tuft of hairs on one (beard).
Leaves: Toothed, opposite, ovate to lanceolate, clasping stem, 2 - 5 in. long, basal rosettes ovate and stalked. Smooth stem.
Habitat: Fields, open woods, meadows, wood edges, exposed cliffs and banks.
Culture: Ordinary, fertile, well-drained acid soil, open sunny exposure.
Propagation: Seeds sown in fall or early spring. Stem cuttings. Division of crowns. Basal rosette develops after flowering.

202 *Penstemon hirsutus* Page 169

Hairy beardtongue

LS: Perennial HT: 1 - 3 ft. BL: May - July

Flower: Pink, lavender or pale purple or partly white, showy, tubular, corolla 2-lipped (upper lip 2-lobed, lower lip 3-cleft), in slender, open cluster.

Leaves: Opposite, oblong to lance shaped, 2 - 5 in. long. Fine woolly or hairy stem.

Habitat, culture and propagation: Same as *P. digitalis.*

Note: *Penstemon smallii* (beardtongue) has pink to purple flowers and shiny, opposite lanceolate leaves with prominent dark veins. Identification difficult; there are many species of native beardtongues.

154 *Verbascum thapsus* Page 157

Mullein, Flannel plant

LS: Biennial HT: 2 - 7 ft. BL: June - November

Flower: Small, 1/2 in. wide, 5 petals, 5 stamens, light yellow, opening randomly a few at a time on an elongated terminal spike (sometimes branched or distorted).

Leaves: First year—basal rosette with thick oblong leaves 4 - 16 in. long. Second year—stem leaves alternate, stalkless, on stout rough stalk. Leaves covered with fine woolly or velvety hairs, gray green.

Habitat: Roadsides, fields, pastures.

Culture: Sun, rocky or sandy soil, alkaline, dry, full sun or partial shade.

Propagation: Seeds sown in the fall, basal rosette first year, blooms second year. Self-seeding.

Note: An escape from Europe. Dried spikes good for flower arranging.

Spiderwort Family (*Commelinaceae*)

A medium-sized family of watery-stemmed annuals or perennial herbs. Terminal clusters of flowers with 3 rounded petals opening 1 or 2 at a time, 3 green sepals, golden stamens. Leaves linear, alternate, parallel veined. The dayflower has 2 large upper petals, 1 small lower petal.

275 *Tradescantia ohiensis* Page 187

Spiderwort, Trinity

LS: Perennial HT: 1 - 2 ft. BL: April - July

Flower: Bright blue to rose, 3 rounded petals, 1 in. wide, terminal heads, borne over 2 long opposite but unequal leaf-like bracts. One or 2 buds open in morning only, then wilt. Usually several to a cluster.

Leaves: Smooth, long, narrow, stalkless, opposite, whitish bloom on stem and leaves.

Habitat: Woodsides, meadows, roadsides.

Culture: Rich sandy soil, partial shade, moisture, acid.

Propagation: Divide clumps in spring. Root at stem joints.

276 *Tradescantia virginiana* Page 187

Spiderwort

LS: Perennial HT: 1 - 2 ft. BL: April - July

Flower: Violet blue, 3 rounded petals, 1 in. wide, showy yellow stamens, borne in terminal cluster over 2 long unequal narrow leaf-like bracts.

Leaves: Long, linear, pointed, folded lengthwise, opposite, hairy, up to 1 ft. long.
Habitat, culture and propagation: Same as *T. chinesis*.

299 *Commelina communis* Page 193
Dayflower, Wandering Jew
LS: Annual HT: 1 - 2 ft. BL: June - October
Flower: Two bright blue upper petals, 1 lower smaller petal, white and inconspicuous, 1/2 in. wide, yellow stamens and anthers. Open for 1 day only in the mornings.
Leaves: Heart-shaped, enfolding bract or spathe just below bloom. Other leaves fleshy, lanceolate, 3 - 5 in. long, alternate, sheathing. Jointed stems. Branching, spreading habit.

Commelina erecta
Dayflower
LS: Perennial HT: 1 - 3 ft. BL: June - October
Flower: Two larger blue petals, 1 smaller white petal.
Leaves: Lanceolate to 6 in. long.

Commelina virginica
Dayflower
LS: Perennial HT: 2 - 4 ft. BL: June - October
Flower: Petals totally blue, fairly large—to 1 in. across.
Leaves: Lanceolate to 8 in. long.
Habitat: (all species) Roadsides, wet woods, moist banks, rock outcrops, sandy openings.
Culture: (all species) Sandy soil, moist, shade.
Propagation: (all species) Root where branches touch ground. Division. Sow seed early in spring or fall.
Note: *C. communis*, an escape from Asia, is now frequently naturalized, but tends to be aggressive.

Sedum or Stonecrop Family (*Crassulaceae*)

Succulent herbs or small shrubs, mostly perennial. Flowers are 4 - 5 petaled, small and clustered. Leaves fleshy or succulent, stalkless.

203 *Sedum telephium* Page 169
Live forever, American orpine
LS: Annual HT: 8 - 15 in. BL: July - September
Flower: Pink to white, small, 1/3 in., 5 pointed petals, star-like, borne in flat conspicuous corymbs 2 - 4 in. wide.
Leaves: Oblong, fleshy, 1 - 2 in. long, alternate, coarsely toothed. Succulent stalks often purplish.
Habitat: Roadsides, open woods, fields, cliffs, rocky outcroppings.
Culture: Full sun or light shade, ordinary soil.
Propagation: Seed. Self seeding.
Note: *Sedum sarmentosum*, a commonly cultivated Asian species with masses of bright yellow flowers and leaves in threes, is often seen clambering over walls and rocks. Our

native species, *Sedum ternatum*, has white flowers with leaves in threes and prefers sandstone and limestone rock.

Spurge Family (*Euphorbiaceae*)

Herbs, shrubs and trees with small, inconspicuous flowers, usually associated with colorful bracts or appendages, stamen 1 to many. Leaves alternate, stipulate, simple. Stem exudes milky juice, often poisonous or irritating, causing skin dermatitis.

59 *Euphorbia corollata* Page 133
Flowering spurge
LS: Perennial HT: 1 - 3 ft. BL: May - October
Flower: In cup-like clusters or cyathia 1/4 in. in diameter, with 5 white petal-like appendages (bracts that surround cluster of minute true center flowers), numerous, clusters are loose and branching.
Leaves: Oblong to linear, slender, up to 1 1/2 in long, blunt tipped, sessile, whorled at base of infloresence, alternate lower down stem, smooth, gray-green.
Habitat: Roadsides, open woodlands, fields.
Culture: Dry, acid soil.
Propagation: Seed.

230 *Euphorbia cyathophora* (often known as *Euphorbia heterophylla* in cultivation.) Page 176
Wild poinsettia, Mexican fire plant, Fire on the mountain, Painted leaf
LS: Annual HT: 10 - 24 in. BL: August - September
Flower: In cup-like clusters or cyathia, with greenish oblong glands as appendages.
Leaves: Glaborus, alternate midstream, varying in shape (lobed to fiddleshaped), small to large red patches on base of upper leaves.
Habitat: Open waste places, woodland clearings.
Culture: Sandy soil.
Propagation: Seed.

60 *Euphorbia marginata* Page 133
Snow-on-the-mountain
LS: Annual HT: 1 - 3 ft. BL: June - October
Flower: In cup-like, very small, inconspicuous clusters or cyathia with 5 white bract-like appendages, terminal clusters borne just above circle of bracts.
Leaves: Oblong, alternate, 1 - 3 in. long. Upper bracts have prominent and broad white margins, branching habit.
Habitat: Hillsides, open woods, roadsides.
Culture: Ordinary soil, sun.
Propagation: Seed planted in spring or fall.
Note: Native to American midwest but widely cultivated in southeast.

St. Johns-Wort Family (*Hyperiaceae*)

Shrubs or herbs, rarely trees. Flowers solitary or in cymes. Petals separate. Many stamens. Leaves opposite or whorled, simple.

Hypericum perforatum
St. Johns-wort
LS: Perennial HT: 1 - 2 ft. BL: June - September
Flower: Golden yellow, 5 petals, numerous conspicuous stamens, to 3/4 in. wide, in terminal cymes; sepals and petals with conspicuous black dots.
Leaves: Speckled with translucent dots (appear perforated), sessile, oblong, small, opposite. Much branched.
Habitat: Fields, roadsides, open woods.
Culture: Loamy or sandy soil, semi-shade.
Propagation: Seed or division.
Note: An escape from Europe. Tends to be aggressive.

Touch-me-not Family (*Balsaminaceae*)

Annual and perennial succulent herbs. Flowers pendant, bright, irregular, 3 - 5 sepals (2 small, large one is petal-like with a curved spur), 5 petals (2 lateral pairs and one helmet-shaped), 5 stamens, superior ovary. Leaves simple, thin, alternate. Exudes watery juice.

172 *Impatiens capensis* Page 161
Jewel weed, Spotted touch-me-not
LS: Annual HT: 2 - 5 ft. BL: July - October
Flower: Orange, spotted reddish brown, 1 in. long, irregular, 5 petals (flaring) and 3 sepals (1 projecting backward forming a long sac with a hollow hook or spur on the end), borne on slender pendulous pedicels from leaf axils. Appear to hang from stem by its middle.
Leaves: Oval, 2 - 3 in. long, light green, alternate, coarsely toothed. Translucent stems, succulent, "bleed" when broken. Many branched.

155 *Impatiens pallida* Page 157
Pale touch-me-not, Snapweed
LS: Annual HT: 2 - 5 ft. BL: July - October
Flower: Pale yellow, spur shorter than *I. capensis*. Spur points downward, 1 1/2 in. long, borne on slender pendulous pedicels from leaf axils.
Leaves: 1 - 4 in., oval, light green, toothed, alternate. Stem as above.
Habitat: (both species) Wet woods, meadows, along streams, marshes, ravines.
Culture: (both species) Alkaline to neutral soil, shade, moisture.
Propagation: (both species) Seed.
Note: Attract butterflies and hummingbirds.

Vervain Family (*Verbenaceae*)

Herbs, shrubs, trees and woody vines. Flowers small, 5 flat petals united to a corolla tube, 5 unequal sepals, 4 stamens (2 shorter), borne in slender spikes or flat clusters. Usually showy. Leaves toothed, simple, opposite.

204 *Verbena canadensis* Page 169
Rose verbena, Rose vervain
LS: Perennial HT: 6 - 18 in. BL: April - October
Flower: Rose, reddish-purple, lilac or white; tubular with flaring corolla lobes, 5 petals, 4 stamens, 1/2 - 3/4 in. wide; borne in dense, terminal, flat-topped cluster.
Leaves: Ovate to lanceolate, to 4 in. long, opposite, palmately veined, coarsely toothed, hairy, spreading habit.
Habitat: Sandy fields and roadsides, rocky ledges.
Culture: Sunny, open exposure; sandy or rocky soil.
Propagation: Seeds, division, cuttings.

277 *Verbena rigida* Page 188
Stiff verbena, Vervain
LS: Perennial HT: 8 - 18 in. BL: March - October
Flower: Lavender, purple or white, small, 5 petals, borne in dense clusters 1 - 2 1/2 in. wide.
Leaves: Hairy, lanceolate, clasping, coarsely serrate, opposite.
Habitat, Culture, Propagation: Same as *V. canadensis.*

278 *Verbena tenuisecta* Page 188
Moss verbena
LS: Perennial HT: 3 - 4 in. BL: March - October
Flower: Small, lavender, purple or white, 5 petals, in terminal flat top clusters.
Leaves: Opposite, deltoid, deeply segmented, fernlike, stems branch abundantly, prostrate.
Habitat: Roadsides, fields, pastures.
Culture: Sandy soil.
Propagation: Seeds (bloom first year). Cuttings. Stems root at nodes. Division.
Note: The latter two verbenas are native to South America and are widely naturalized in our area.

Violet Family (*Violaceae*)

Perennial herbs and shrubs. Flowers irregular, 5 sepals, 5 petals, lower one usually wider, may extend back into a spur, lateral petals usually bearded. Leaves simple and heart-shaped.

Viola
Violet
LS: Perennial HT: 2 - 16 in. BL: March - May
More than 100 species in the United States. Approximately 3/4 are blue or purplish.

Flower: Bilaterally symmetrical, 5 sepals (separate), 5 petals (separate). Two upper petals, 2 side wings and 1 flat lower petal combine to make up flower, lower one often lowest and bearing a backward projecting spur.
Leaves: Alternate, simple but sometimes deeply lobed.
"Stemmed"—leaves and flowers on same stalk; leaves appear on aboveground stem.
"Stemless"—flowers and leaves on separate stalks; leaves appear basal.

61 *Viola blanda* Page 134
Sweet white violet
Flower: Small, dainty, short-stemmed fragrant white flowers, lower petals purple veined. Stemless.
Leaves: Ovate, reddish stalks, underground stems and runners.
Habitat: Moist, rich woods.

62 *Viola canadensis* Page 134
Canada violet
Flower: Fragrant, white, yellow at base of petals which are streaked purple-brown. Stemmed.
Leaves: Finely toothed, slender purple stalk.
Habitat: Rich woods. Form tall, bushy clump.

279 *Viola conspersa* Page 188
Dog violet
Flower: Light lilac-purple or blue, small, 3/4 in. wide with narrow and curved spur about 1/5 in. long. Stemmed.
Leaves: 1 - 2 in. long, heart-shaped, slightly scalloped, erect tufted stems.
Habitat: Rich, damp woods, meadows, often along streams.

156 *Viola hastata* Page 157
Halberd-leaved violet, Spear-leaved violet
Flower: Small, about 1/2 - 3/4 in. across, yellow, dark purple veins, light beard, very short spur, stemmed.
Leaves: 2 - 3 in. long, triangular, heart-shaped at base, toothed, sometimes mottled.
Habitat: Rich deciduous woods.

280 *Viola hirsutula* Page 188
Southern wood violet
Flower: Deep violet. Stemless.
Leaves: Purplish, silvery and downy below. Hairy.
Habitat: Woods.

281 *Viola pedata* Page 189
Birdfoot violet
Flower: Deep blue to lilac (lower petal veined with violet), orange anthers. Upper 2 petals may occasionally be darker. Stemless.
Leaves: Deeply cut and palmate (resembling a bird's foot).
Habitat: Roadsides, fields, slopes.

157 *Viola pubescens* (sometimes called *Viola eriocarpa*) Page 158
Downy yellow violet
Flower: Yellow, 3 lower petals have dark purple veins. Side petals bearded. Stemmed.
Leaves: Heart-shaped, hairy. Downy stem.
Habitat: Rich deciduous woods.
Note: Other yellow violets: *Viola tripartita*—leaves cleft into 3 lobes. *Viola rotundfolia* has yellow (veined brown) flowers and round leaves. Stemless.

282 *Viola rafinesquii*, (sometimes listed with European *Viola kitaibelliana*) Page 189
Johnny jump up, Field pansy
LS: Annual
Flower: Small, white, blue or purple with yellow eye. Lower 3 petals have purple veins.
Leaves: Cut into narrow segments, giving a feathery appearance. Slender stems, erect.
Habitat: Roadsides, fields.

63, *Viola sororia* (includes *Viola papilionacea*) Pages 134, 189
283 Common blue, Butterfly violet
Flower: Blue to white. Stemless.
Leaves: Large, heart-shaped with scalloped margins.
Habitat: Woods, roadsides, fields, slopes.
Culture: (all species) Most grow from a thick rhizome in rich, humus-filled soil, slightly acid, in partial shade. The birdfoot violet prefers dry uplands, sand and an acid soil.
Propagation: (all species) Seed (most self seeding). Transplant at any time with a good ball of soil. Keep moist.
Note: There is some dispute about taxonomic distinctions of stemless blue violets. The stemless Confederate violet with gray blue somewhat streaked flowers may be treated as a color form of *Viola sororia*; it is not a distinct species but may be sold as *Viola priceana*.

Waterleaf Family (*Hydrophyllaceae*)

Herbs or rarely shrubs, flower usually arranged along one side of the branches or at the tips of stems in coils like fiddlesticks.

284 *Phacelia bipinnafida* Page 189
Scorpion weed
LS: Biennial HT: 1 - 2 ft. BL: April - June
Flower: Five sepals and 5 petals united, numerous, lavender blue, round, 1/2 - 1 in. in diameter, buds in coiled clusters and straighten as flowers mature.
Leaves: Light green, may be mottled, pinnately divided into 5 deeply lobed segments, loose branching habit.
Habitat: Rich woods, rocky places.
Culture: Rich, loose organic and moist soil, shade.
Propagation: Seeds (often self seeding). Transplant seedlings. Showy when planted in masses.

Water Lily Family (*Nymphaeaceae*)

Aquatic plants growing from large rhizome. Flowers large, showy, solitary, borne on separate stalk, 3 - 6 sepals, petals and stamens range from 3 to numerous. Leaves large, peltate or cordate, floating, long petioled.

64 *Nymphaea odorata* Page 134

American water lily, Sweet water lily

LS: Perennial HT: 3 - 6 ft. BL: June - September

Flower: White or pale pink with yellow stamen, solitary, many lanceolate petals, 3 - 6 in. wide. Bloom early in the morning, closing at noon. Fragrant.

Leaves: (lily pads), rounded and flat, notched at base to center, green on top, purple below, 4 - 12 in. wide. Floating on water (from submerged thick horizontal rootstock).

Habitat: Slow moving, shallow, quiet water. Fresh. Warm.

Culture: Deep rich mud, covered with 2 ft. of water, very acid, full sun, warm water.

Propagation: Transplant in spring. Divide roots in fall. Seed. Spread rapidly.

Wintergreen or Pryola Family (*Pryolaceae*)

Evergreen perennial herbs growing from creeping rhizomes. Flowers nodding, 4 - 5 petals, 4 - 5 sepals, 8 - 10 stamens, solitary or in racemes. Leaves mostly evergreen, opposite, simple, sometimes scales. Color may not be green. Sometimes root parasites.

65 *Chimaphila maculata* Page 135

Spotted wintergreen, Striped pipsissewa

LS: Perennial HT: 4 - 6 in. BL: June - August

Flower: White, 5-petaled, cup-shaped, borne in terminal pendant umbels, waxy, thick substance, fragrant.

Leaves: Lanceolate, toothed, almost whorled, in tiers, leathery dark green mottled white along veins, evergreen, 1 - 2 in. long, pointed at tip.

Habitat: Dry coniferous woods.

Culture: Shade, dry, very acid soil, well-drained and mulched. May rely on fungi at roots for food supply.

Propagation: Softwood stem cuttings rooted in sand. Division of underground stems. Does not transplant well.

158 *Monotropa hypopithys* Page 158

Pinesap, False beech drops

LS: Parasite HT: 5 - 8 in. BL: June - September

Flower: Several, small drooping red-orange or dully yellow, vaselike, clustered in a raceme. Bract-like sepals, wedge-shaped petals form bell-shaped flower, become erect when seed develops.

Leaves: Scalelike, same color as flower, alternate.

Monotropa uniflora
Indian pipe, Ghost plant
LS: Parasite HT: 5 - 8 in. BL: June - September
Flower: Single, small, nodding, white (occasionally light pink or blue), bract-like sepals, wedge-shaped petals form bell-shaped flower. Waxy. Turn upright as seeds form.
Leaves: Scalelike, same color as flowers, clasping, alternate.
Habitat: (both species) Oak, beech and pine woods.
Culture: (both species) Damp, shade, acid, humus, leaf mold. Parasite associated with roots of oaks, beech or pine trees. Usually grow in clusters.
Propagation: (both species) Parasite—live on root fungi and decayed vegetable matter in the soil.

Wood Sorrel Family (*Oxalidaceae*)

Annual and perennial herbs. Flowers have 5 petals, 5 sepals, 5 - 10 stamens. Leaves alternate, clover like (divided into heart-shaped leaflets). Grow from rhizomes or tubers.

205 *Oxalis montana* (sometimes placed with *Oxalis acetosella*) Page 170
Common wood sorrel
LS: Perennial HT: 3 - 6 in. BL: May - July
Flower: White or pink with deep pink veins and eye, 5 notched petals, 3/4 in. wide, 10 stamens, solitary, dainty.
Leaves: Cloverlike, sometimes blotched. Close at night.

285 *Oxalis violacea* Page 190
Violet wood sorrel
LS: Perennial HT: 4 - 8 in. BL: May - July
Flower: Five flaring petals, 5 green sepals, rose purple or purple violet, borne in clusters on leafless stalk, 3/4 in. wide, delicate.
Leaves: Palmately compound, heart-shaped leaflets arranged cloverlike, fold along center crease, reddish underneath. Close at night.
Habitat: (both species) Open woods, banks.
Culture: (both species) Sun, moist humus-rich soil.
Propagation: (both species) Seed. Division of runners or bulbs.
Note: Three yellow varieties (*Oxalis europaea, Oxalis stricta* and *Oxalis corniculata*) have yellow flowers 1/2 in. wide.

FERNS AND FERN ALLIES

Club Moss Family (*Lycopodiaceae*)

Fern ally. Rhizomatous herbs. Plants resemble giant mosses with evergreen simple leaves, never divided, scalelike, creeping stems, one type of spore produced terminally in club-shaped structures.

303 *Lycopodium digitatum* (sometimes listed as *Lycopodium complanatum* or *Lycopodium flabelliforme*) Page 194
Ground-cedar, Running-pine, Christmas green
LS: Perennial HT: 6 - 8 in.
Leaves: Tiny, cedar-like scales, grown together for more than half their length; numerous, evergreen, creeping stems, irregularly and much branched; fan-shaped branchlets flattened but concave on underside. Form minute spores on stalked spikes.
Habitat: Roadsides, thickets, edges of pine woodlands, dry oak-pine woods.
Culture: Dry partially-shaded rich woodlands with pine straw litter, acid to nearly neutral soil.
Propagation: By division of rhizomes (difficult to transplant). Increase by cuttings.
Note: Good for groundcover. Wide destruction by use as Christmas decorations; whole populations should never be eliminated.

Horsetail Family (*Equisetaceae*)

Fern ally. Rhizomatous herbs. Upright stems jointed at nodes with hollow center. Leaves scalelike, minute and fused together into a sheath.

Equisetum arvense
Horsetail rush, Field horsetail
LS: Perennial HT: 1 - 2 ft.
Leaves: No true leaves (scales at joints). Stem rush-like, striped, hollow jointed, sometimes branching in whorls on green sterile stems; fertile stems pinkish with terminal spore cluster. Above ground stems are produced annually.
Habitat: Fields, banks, woods, roadsides.
Culture: Damp, sandy neutral soil, semi-shade.
Propagation: Division of creeping rootstock. Tends to be aggressive.
Note: Good for flower arranging.

304 *Equisetum hyemale* Page 194
Scouring rush, Common horsetail
LS: Perennial HT: 3 - 4 ft.
Leaves: No true leaves (scales at joints). Stems are unbranched, rush-like and evergreen with black bands near joints.
Habitat: Pond margins and seepy disturbed areas.
Culture: Damp, sandy shaded slopes.
Propagation: Division of rootstock.

Osmunda Family (*Osmundaceae*)

"Flowering" ferns—spore masses have no fruit covers; spores are greenish.

305 *Osmunda cinnamomea* Page 195
Cinnamon fern
LS: Perennial HT: 1 - 3 ft.
Leaves: Large, coarse, lanceolate, woolly in spring. Leaflets narrow, lance-shaped,

pointed, deeply cut, 20 or more pairs nearly opposite. In midsummer a spiked stalk with brown spore cases appear in the center of the fronds. Deciduous.
Habitat: Ditches, ravines, slopes.
Culture: Moist rich deciduous woodsy soil, acid, shade or diffused light, good drainage.
Propagation: Root division.

306 *Osmunda regalis* (var. *spectabilis*) Page 195
Royal fern, Flowering fern
LS: Perennial HT: 15 - 30 in.
Leaves: Foliage pale green in sunlight or bright green in less light, rounded leaflets, opposite and widely spaced, 6 or more pairs. Sub-leaflets alternate, narrow, oblong, bases cordate or rounded, 8 or more pairs plus terminal. Fronds clustered, shrublike. Deciduous. Stalk—tall, straw colored, reddish at base.
Habitat: Along streams, meadows, thickets.
Culture: Moist rich soil, filtered to full sun.
Propagation: Division. Spores. Fertile portion of frond borne on tip.

Polypody Family (*Polypodiaceae*)

Ferns. Sporecase rings vertical and interrupted by the stalk. Some species have fruit dots on underside or under margins of fertile leaves.

307 *Adiantum pedatum* Page 195
Maidenhair fern
LS: Perennial HT: 12 - 18 in.
Leaves: Compound or palmate, bluish green, 5 or 6 on each branch (made up of several sub-leaflets varying in size and shape), elongated. Slender, erect stalks, black. Deciduous.
Habitat: Ravines, rocky banks, slopes.
Culture: Rich woodsy soil, shade or diffused light, alkaline, good drainage, moisture.
Propagation: By root division. Do not cover too deeply.

308 *Asplenium platyneuron* Page 195
Ebony spleenwort fern
LS: Perennial HT: 1 ft.
Leaves: Fronds tall and narrow, tapering at top and bottom. Dark green. Eighteen or more pairs of leaflets. Leaflets alternate, narrow, oblong, eared at base, serrated edges. Ladder-like pattern. Sterile fronds shorter, pendant (may be prostrate). Semi-evergreen. Stalk dark brown, almost black, stiff, erect.
Habitat: Shaded woods, fields, banks.
Culture: Well-drained rocky soil, sun or shade, moist.
Propagation: Spores or division. May colonize.

309 *Athyrium asplenioides* Page 196
Southern lady fern
LS: Perennial HT: 1 - 2 ft.
Leaves: Broad, lance-shaped, cut into pairs of not opposite upward pointed leaflets, up to 8 in. long, cut again into sub-leaflets. Lower pair of leaflets usually horizontal.

Deciduous. Scattered dark scales on stalk. Feathery, lacy fronds. Grows in circular clusters.
Habitat: Ravines, slopes, under trees.
Culture: Moist, rich soil. Semi-shade.
Propagation: By root division.
Note: Good for natualizing because of texture, size and color.

310 *Onoclea sensibilis* Page 196
Sensitive fern, Bead fern
LS: Perennial HT: 1 - 2 ft.
Leaves: Light green, scattered white hairs underneath, leathery, coarse, 12 nearly opposite pairs of almost triangular leaflets, upper ones winged with minor tapering near axis, lower leaflets widely spaced, lowest or next to lowest pair of leaflets the longest and tapering at both ends, wavy margins, prominent network forming veins, depressed. Fertile spikes short-branched and beadlike. Long stalk, yellow, brown and thickened at base.
Habitat: Banks, woodsides, meadows.
Culture: Damp soil, full sun or shade.
Propagation: Spores. Division. Dies back at first frost.

311 *Polystichum acrostichoides* Page 196
Christmas fern
LS: Perennial HT: 12 - 18 in.
Leaves: Simple (once cut), leaflets lustrous rich green, lance-shaped, eared on one side at axis, short-stemmed, fronds taper up and down from the middle. Fronds coarse, rigid, leathery, form circular cluster from a central rootstock; sterile leaves stay evergreen during the winter, 2 lower leaflets almost opposite, horizontal and deflexed, middle leaflets alternate and horizontal. Stalk brown at base, green above, scaly.
Habitat: Rocky shaded slopes, stream banks, ravines.
Culture: Prefers rich rocky or sandy soil, alkaline, shade or semi-shade.
Propagation: Spores or division. Tends to grow in colonies.
Note: Individual leaflet looks like a Christmas stocking when turned vertically or like a sleigh when turned horizontally.

312 *Pteridium aquilinum* Page 196
Bracken fern
LS: Perennial HT: 12 - 20 in.
Leaves: Thrice cut. Fronds dark green, triangular shaped, almost horizontal, coarse, 3 almost equal sections, 2 lower sections nearly opposite, stemmed. Leaflets oblong, cut into sub-leaflets (close together, variable shapes). Tall stalk, green, smooth, rigid.
Habitat: Woods, pastures, thickets.
Culture: Full sun or shade. Grows in poor soil.
Propagation: Spores or division. Colonizes. Dies back after first frost.

313 *Thelypteris hexagonophtera* Page 197
Broad beech fern
LS: Perennial HT: 12 - 18 in.
Leaves: Light green, triangular, tilts backwards. Leaflets long, narrow with long pointed tips, semi-winged along stem, opposite, lowest pair droop downward and outward (not

winged), cut almost to mid-vein into 18 segments. Stalk scaly and hairy.
Habitat: Cliffs, ravines, shaded banks, along streams.
Culture: Semi-shade, rich, moist woodlands.
Propagation: Spores or division. Colonizes.

314 *Thelypteris noveboracensis* Page 197
New York fern
LS: Perennial HT: 8 - 20 in.
Leaves: Fronds yellow green, blade up to 4 in. wide in middle tapering on top and bottom. Leaflets long and thin, cut nearly to midvein, delicate texture, never opposite. Lower leaflets very small. Deciduous. Stalk smooth and light green, brown and scaly at base.
Habitat: Open mixed woods.
Culture: Moist, rich, well-drained soil, full or half sun.
Propagation: Spores. Division of rhizomes. Colonizes.

SHRUBS AND TREES

Bedstraw Family (*Rubiaceae*)

Cephalanthus occidentalis
Button bush
LS: Perennial shrub HT: 5 - 12 ft. BL: July - September
Flower: Small, tubular, white, borne in dense showy and fuzzy ball-like clusters at branch tips and from leaf axils. Fragrant.
Leaves: Simple, opposite (sometimes 3 - 4 whorled), oval, 3 - 5 in. long, elliptic, deep green, glossy. Deciduous. Spreading branches.
Habitat: Moist places, bogs and swamps.
Culture: Sun or shade, moisture, good garden soil.
Propagation: By seeds or cuttings.

Buckthorn Family (*Rhamnaceae*)

Deciduous shrubs, small trees or vines. Flowers usually in axillary clusters, umbels or racemes, small and regular. Leaves alternate or opposite, pinnately nerved with conspicuous parallel veins.

66 *Ceanothus americanus* Page 135
New Jersey tea, Red root
LS: Perennial shrub HT: 2 - 3 ft. BL: May - August
Flower: Dense, flat-topped or rounded showy clusters, formed of small, white blooms with 5 petals.
Leaves: Alternate, oval, 1 - 3 in. long, finely toothed margins, 3 prominent veins. Deciduous.
Habitat: Roadsides, open hills, and woods.
Culture: Dry, sandy soil.
Propagation: Seed.

Calycanthus Family (*Calycanthaceae*)

A small family of hardy deciduous or evergreen shrubs with fragrant axillary or solitary reddish-brown flowers, many bract-like sepals and petals and numerous stamens. Leaves opposite, entire, oblong or ovate.

Calycanthus fertilis
Smooth allspice
LS: Perennial shrub HT: 5 - 10 ft. BL: April - June
Flower: Brownish, without much odor. Otherwise similar to *C. floridus*. Fruits fleshy.
Leaves: Deciduous, oval, sharp-tipped, smooth and whitish beneath, 4 - 6 in. long. Bushier than *C. floridus*.
Habitat: Open woods or woody areas.
Culture: Rich soil, moist, well-drained, shade or semi-shade.
Propagation: Seeds, division. Suckers.
Note: Seeds said to be poisonous. Sometimes lumped with next species or placed as a variety with it; seems distinct in garden setting.

231 *Calycanthus floridus* Page 176
Sweet shrub, Carolina allspice
LS: Perennial shrub HT: 3 - 8 ft. BL: April - June
Flower: Deep maroon—1 1/2 in. in diameter, very aromatic. Similar petals and sepals form a cup-like bloom. Fig-shaped fruits contain many seed.
Leaves: Oval, pointed, deciduous, aromatic, densely hairy and pale beneath.
Habitat: Moist rich woods, slopes, creek banks.
Culture: Acid soil.
Propagation: Sow seeds when ripened. Plant spreads by underground parts. Divide. Move small plants.
Note: The curious fruits of sweet shrubs resemble insect cocoons and are attacked by birds that peck out holes allowing seeds to drop.

Dogwood Family (*Cornaceae*)

Trees and shrubs. Flowers small, inconspicuous, tightly packed, and greenish, some species with showy white bracts. Leaves simple, usually opposite with conspicuous parallel lateral veins and sticky sap.

67 *Cornus florida* Page 135
Flowering dogwood
LS: Perennial shrub HT: 5 - 25 ft. BL: April
Flower: Flat clusters of small blooms (yellow green and inconspicuous) surrounded by 4 long and showy white bracts (often mistakenly called petals), a touch of brownish-red on their blunt and notched tips. Blooms appear before leaves emerge. Clusters of fleshy red berry-like fruit appear after flowering. Flower buds conspicuous all winter.
Leaves: Opposite, simple, oval, 3 - 5 in. long. Deciduous. Turn scarlet to dark purple in fall. Spreading branches.
Habitat: Woods, beneath taller trees, roadsides near trees.

Culture: Partial shade, sheltered from wind, average soil. Floriferousness increases with more sun.
Propagation: Move only small trees with a large ball of soil. Keep well watered. Seed sown in fall germinate next year.
Note: Pruning in late summer or fall removes next year's bloom. Prune just after flowering.

68 *Cornus stricta* (formerly *Cornus foemina*) Page 135
Stiff dogwood
LS: Perennial shrub HT: 15 ft. BL: April
Flower: Inconspicuous, very small, 4 petals, whitish, borne in flat or round-topped clusters, 2 - 3 in. across.
Leaves: Opposite, simple, green on both sides but paler underneath, elliptic, 2 - 5 in. long, deciduous, twigs red or brown, pith white.
Habitat: Woods.
Culture: Ordinary garden soil, acid.
Propagation: Seeds, cuttings of mature wood, layering.
Note: Similar species *Cornus amomum* (silky dogwood) has similar flower with a more rounded cluster. Twigs are dull purple and have a brown pith. Leaves have rounded bases. Blooms in May - June, same time as the elderberry.

Heath Family

206 *Kalmia latifolia* Page 170
Mountain laurel, Calico bush, Mountain ivy
LS: Perennial shrub HT: 3 - 8 ft. BL: May - June
Flower: Buds pink, flowers pink to white, cup-shaped, borne in showy terminal clusters. Flower stalks and sepals glandular and sticky. Anthers fit in pockets of corolla and spring out to spread pollen.
Leaves: Evergreen, smooth and glossy, oval or elliptic, pointed on both ends, 2 - 5 in. long, leathery texture. Many branches.
Habitat: Woods.
Culture: Sandy or rocky soil, acid.
Propagation: Seed. Transplant small plants. Hardy and easy to grow.

69 *Leucothoe axillaris* Page 136
Fetterbush, Coastal sweetbells
LS: Perennial shrub HT: 3 - 6 ft. BL: April - June
Flower: Small, bell-shaped, white, in clusters in leaf axils.
Leaves: Leathery, shiny, evergreen, elliptical.

70 *Leucothoe fontanesiana* (formerly *Leucothoe catesbaei*) Page 136
Dog Hobble, Fetterbush, Drooping Leucothoe
LS: Perennial shrub HT: 3 - 7 ft. BL: April - June
Flower: Creamy white, waxy, bell shaped, fragrant, borne in dense showy, drooping clusters 2 - 3 in. long, along stems and at tips of branches.
Leaves: Dark, shiny green, evergreen but turn bronze in winter, leathery, oval, alternate, 3 - 4 in. long. Graceful arching branches.

Habitat: (both species) Wooded areas, along streams.
Culture: (both species) Shade or partial sun, moist peaty soil supplied with humus, acid, protect from wind. Shallow rooted, require mulching.
Propagation: (both species) By division in very early spring or late fall. Layering, softwood cuttings or by seed.

71 *Lyonia mariana* Page 136
Stagger bush
LS: Perennial shrub HT: 4 - 6 ft. BL: May - June
Flower: Urn-shaped, white or pinkish, about 1/2 in. long, in nodding racemes at leaf joints on older branches.
Leaves: Simple, alternate, elliptical to oval, 1 - 2 in. long, deciduous.
Habitat: Open coniferous woods.
Culture: Sandy or peaty loam, acid soil, partial shade. Mulch with dry leaves.
Propagation: Seeds, layering, cuttings.
Note: The technical separation of *Lyonia* from *Leucothoe* is by the mature fruit, which has corklike thickenings where it splits in *Lyonia*. Otherwise, these two genera with weeping to arching branches, the leaves protruding from both sides, are look-alikes.

72 *Oxydendrum arboreum* Page 136
Sourwood
LS: Perennial tree HT: 10 - 50 ft. BL: June
Flower: Creamy white, delicate, urn-shaped, 1/4 - 1/2 in. long, borne in showy drooping and plumelike 1-sided clusters 5 - 8 in. long, fragrant, fruits are dry bell-shaped capsules.
Leaves: Oblong, alternate, finely serrated, dull green turning brilliant red in autumn, 4 - 8 in. long, deciduous. The best distinguishing feature is the underside mid-vein which bears sparse but conspicuous stiff hairs.
Habitat: Upland woods or wood edges, disturbed banks.
Culture: Ordinary garden soil, sun.
Propagation: Transplant seedlings. Slow growing in cultivation.
Note: Blooms attract honeybees.

73 *Pieris floribunda* Page 137
Mountain fetterbush
LS: Perennial shrub HT: 3 - 4 ft. BL: April - May
Flower: Nodding, fragrant, small, white, urn-shaped, upright terminal 3 - 4 in. showy panicles. Flower buds obvious all winter.
Leaves: Dull green, elliptic to oval, 1 1/2 - 3 in. long, pointed, alternate, leathery, sparsely toothed. Evergreen (may be bronze in winter).
Habitat: Sheltered spots, slopes.
Culture: Peaty, moist sandy, moderately acid soil, sun or partial shade. Keep mulched with oak or beech leaves.
Propagation: Seeds or layering. Always move with ball of soil, securely wrapped. Slow growing. Tends to bloom profusely and earlier than other fetterbushes.

74 *Vaccinium arboreum* Page 137
Farkleberry, sparkleberry
LS: Perennial shrub HT: 15 - 20 ft. BL: April - June
Flower: Tiny, white, bell-shaped, 1/4 in. long. Berries: Black, shiny, edible but dryish.

Leaves: 1/2 - 2 in. long, shiny, elliptic to rounded, evergreen to semi-evergreen. Turn deep red to crimson in fall.
Habitat: Upland woods.
Culture: Ordinary soil.
Propagation: Seed. One of the most common shrubs in Georgia.

Vaccinium ashei
Rabbit-eye blueberry
LS: Perennial shrub HT: 5 - 15 ft. BL: April - June
Flower: Similar to *V. corymbosum*.
Leaves: Often hairy below, sometimes bluish green.
Habitat: Upland woods.
Culture: Ordinary soil. More tolerant of South Georgia summers. Most cultivated blueberries in Georgia were derived from this common wild species.
Propagation: Same as *V. arboreum*.

Vaccinium angustifolium
Low sweet blueberry
LS: Perennial shrub HT: 1 - 2 ft. BL: April - June
Flower: Similar to *V. corymbosum*.
Leaves: Similar to *V. corymbosum*.
Habitat, Culture and Propagation: Similar to *V. corymbosum*.

75 *Vaccinium corymbosum* Page 137
Highbush blueberry
LS: Perennial shrub HT: 5 - 10 ft. BL: April - June
Flower: Small, white to pink, urn-shaped flowers in short terminal clusters. Berries: blue, edible.
Leaves: 1 - 2 in. long, entire, elliptic, shrubby habit. Turn bronzy red in fall. Deciduous.
Habitat: Pine woodlands, swamps.
Culture: Acid soil (absolute must), sandy, well- drained, dry, shade.
Propagation: By seeds, cuttings or division.

Vaccinium stamineum
Deerberry
LS: Perennial shrub HT: 5 - 10 ft. BL: April - June
Flower: Similar to *V. arboreum*, flowers open, bell-shaped, stamens longer than petals. Berries: Greenish, dry.
Leaves: Oblong, variable, often blue green, white below, up to 4 in. long, usually hairy.
Habitat: Upland woods.
Culture: Average soil.
Propagation: Seeds.
Note: Conspicuous shrub with greenish fairly large (almost 1/2 in. in diameter) pithy fruit; commonly browsed by deer. Blueberries have many soft tiny seeds. Huckleberries have 10 hard seed and belong to the genus *Gaylussacia* that is rare in cultivation.

Rhododendron-Deciduous Types

Azalea—Honeysuckle
LS: Perennial shrubs
Flower: Irregular, slightly 2-lipped, tube length varying, vase, trumpet or funnel shaped with slender petals and elongated corolla tube, 5 long stamens; flowers usually borne in clusters at twig tips.
Leaves: Clustered near twig tips, hairy on edges, alternate, simple, deciduous.

76 *Rhododendron alabamanese* Page 137
Alabama azalea
LS: Perennial shrub HT: 3 - 8 ft. BL: April - May
Flower: White to very pale pink with lemon yellow blotch on upper lobe. Lemony fragrance. Tube longer than lobes.
Leaves: Elliptic to obovate to 2 1/4 in. long.
Habitat: Dry open woodlands, hillsides.

77 *Rhododendron arborescens* Page 138
Smooth, sweet or tree azalea
LS: Perennial shrub HT: 8 - 20 ft. BL: June
Flower: Large, white, sometimes striped pink (often has yellow blotch on upper petal), broad trumpet like flowers, very fragrant. Blooms appear after the leaves.
Leaves: Glossy, deep green, oblong, 1 - 3 in., hairless.
Habitat: Along streams, hillsides.

173 *Rhododendron austrinum* Page 162
Florida azalea
LS: Perennial shrub HT: 5 - 10 ft. BL: March - April
Flower: Funnel-shaped, yellow to orange, borne in large clusters near tips of twigs, very aromatic, flowers before or as leaves expand.
Leaves: Elliptic, 2 - 3 in. long, hairy below, deciduous.
Habitat: Woods, wood edges, along streams.

232 *Rhododendron calendulaceum* Page 176
Flame azalea
LS: Perennial shrub HT: 5 - 10 ft. BL: May - June
Flower: Striking yellow, orange or red; vase shaped, large, up to 2 in. in diameter with 5 - 7 to a cluster. Appear before or with new leaves. Not fragrant.
Leaves: Ovate, 1 - 3 in. long.
Habitat: Open hillsides, along streams.

207 *Rhododendron canescens* Page 170
Hoary azalea, Piedmont azalea, Sweet azalea
LS: Perennial shrub HT: 5 - 15 ft. BL: April
Flower: Deep pink to almost white; fragrant; numerous and small, tightly packed on head. Bell-shaped. Bloom as leaf unfurls.
Leaves: Oblong, 2 - 4 in. long, grayish and hairy beneath.
Habitat: Streams, moist woods, dry ledges.

Rhododendron cumberlandense
Cumberland azalea
LS: Perennial shrub HT: 5 - 9 ft. BL: June
Flower: Small, orange, red or yellow, borne in abundant clusters. Blooms after leaves form.
Leaves: Obovate, to 2 in. long.
Habitat: Open upland woods.

208 *Rhododendron flammeum* (formerly *R. speciosum*) Page 170
Oconee azalea
LS: Perennial shrub HT: 5 - 6 ft. BL: April - May
Flower: Scarlet, salmon, pink, yellow; small but abundant, showy. Not fragrant.
Leaves: Oblong to ovate, to 2 1/4 in. long.
Habitat: Open woods, woody slopes.

209 *Rhododendron periclymenoides* (formerly *R. nudiflorum*) Page 171
Pinxter flower, Pinxterbloom, Honeysuckle
LS: Perennial shrub HT: 2 - 9 ft. BL: April
Flower: Pink to nearly white, funnel-shaped, open before or with leaves; barely fragrant, profuse. Very showy.
Leaves: Thin, ovate, 2 - 3 in. long, pointed on both ends.
Habitat: Dry woods. Will grow in lime soil but prefers acid.

233 *Rhododendron prunifolium* Page 177
Plumleaf azalea, Red honeysuckle
LS: Perennial shrub HT: 5 - 12 ft. BL: July - September
Flower: Red, red-orange, salmon, long-tubed. Non-fragrant, crowded clusters. Outer clusters opening first. Long stamens.
Leaves: Dark green, oblong, smooth (with few, if any, hairs) resembling a plum leaf. Develop before blooms appear.
Habitat: Moist soil, rich wooded ravines, along streams.
Note: Threatened; propagated material available.

210 *Rhododendron vaseyi* Page 171
Pink-shell azalea
LS: Perennial shrub HT: 6 - 15 ft. BL: April - May
Flower: Light rose to clear pink, spotted brownish-orange on upper lobe, borne in clusters, appears before leaves unfold, tube short. Bell shaped.
Leaves: Oblong, 3 - 5 in.
Habitat: Rich woods, along streams, hillsides.

78 *Rhododendron viscosum* Page 138
White swamp azalea, Swamp honeysuckle, Clammy azalea
LS: Perennial shrub HT: 5 - 8 ft. BL: May - June
Flower: Four - nine in a cluster, white or faintly pink, slender tubed, very fragrant, appear after leaves expand. Spicy odor like cloves.
Leaves: Ovate to oblong, 1 - 2 1/2 in. long, glossy, green to white beneath, bristly on margins.
Habitat: Swamps, bogs, near streams.
Culture: (all species) Semi-shade, acid soil, peaty, well-drained (except swamp azalea).
Propagation: (all species) Division. Transplant to save from bulldozers. Prune severely. Cut tops back when not in active growth, preferably in late summer. Transplants well. Do not let roots be exposed to the air and dry out.
Note: Bloom date, fragrance and flower color may aid in identification. Some species tend to hybridize. Difficult to identify because of similarities of different species.

Rhododendron - Evergreen Types

286 *Rhododendron catawbiense* Page 190
Mountain rosebay, Catawba rhododendron, Purple laurel
LS: Perennial shrub HT: 3 - 20 ft. BL: April - June
Flower: Purple-rose, borne in large clusters.
Leaves: Oblong, dark green, pale white beneath, evergreen, thick and leathery; rounded at both ends.

79 *Rhododendron maximum* Page 138
Rosebay, Great laurel
LS: Perennial shrub HT: 6 - 20 ft. BL: May - June
Flower: White to shell pink, cup-shaped, borne in large clusters (smaller than other species), later blooming.
Leaves: Evergreen, large, thick and leathery, dark green above pale orange beneath; tapered at stem end, elliptic.

211 *Rhododendron minus* Page 171
Carolina rhododendron, Piedmont rhododendron
LS: Perennial shrub HT: 4 - 7 ft. BL: April - June
Flower: Light rose pink to magenta, funnel-shaped, in many flowered clusters.
Leaves: Evergreen, rusty and scaly beneath.
Habitat: (all species) Rocky hillsides, slopes, woods, stream banks.
Culture: (all species) Hardy, sun or shade. Acid, deep porous soil, rich in leaf mold and humus. Well-drained. Leaves bend down and roll into tight coils during sub-freezing weather.
Propagation: (all species) Seed. Plant when ripe. Keep moist. Divide clumps in late summer. Plant at same depth as earth line near the base of the plant.
Note: Sometimes a Blue Ridge form is called *R. carolinianum*.

Holly Family (*Aquilifoliaceae*)

Trees and shrubs, inconspicuous greenish-white flowers. Male and female flowers on separate plants. Leaves leathery, alternate, simple, mostly evergreen.

234 *Ilex opaca* Page 177

American holly

LS: Perennial shrub HT: 5 - 25 ft. BL: May - June

Flower: Inconspicuous, small, creamy white, in small clusters borne in leaf axils. Fruit usually solitary, pea-sized, brilliant red.

Leaves: Evergreen, thick, alternate, spiny, elliptic, dull green above, much paler yellow-green beneath, 2 - 4 in. long. Spreading branches.

Habitat: Deciduous woods.

Culture: Acid soil, sun or partial shade. Hardy.

Propagation: Cuttings from ripe wood. Difficult to transplant. Remove most of leaves before digging. Move with large ball of soil, wrapped. Prune severely. Keep moist. Seed germination very slow. Has been over used in decorating and is becoming uncommon in some areas. Male and female flowers on separate plants—essential to have both to assure pollination.

Note: Other native hollies are worthy of consideration for the home garden. The evergreen types are: *Ilex glabra* (inkberry, gallberry) which has lustrous green blunt-tipped foliage and blue-black fruit; *Ilex latifolia* (lusterleaf holly) which has leaves 4 - 7 in. long resembling the magnolia and dull red berries born in clusters; and *Ilex vomitoria* (yaupon) which has small wavy-edged leaves and red fruit. The latter two varieties should be planted in protected spots in northern areas of the state. Deciduous varieties include *Ilex decidua* (passion haw) and *Ilex verticillata* (winterberry) whose foliage turns bright orange before dropping.

Honeysuckle Family (*Caprifoliaceae*)

Small shrubs, trees and vines. Flowers usually bell-shaped, funnel like or tubular. Corolla flaring into 5 lobes (regular or irregular), 5 stamens, usually in cymes. Leaves opposite, simple or compound.

80 *Viburnum acerifolium* Page 138

Mapleleaf viburnum

LS: Perennial shrub HT: 5 - 6 ft. BL: April - May

Flower: Small, borne in flat-topped clusters, cream, 2 - 3 in. across, on long stalks. Fruit dark purple.

Leaves: Three-lobed (resembling a maple leaf), coarsely toothed, hairy beneath, opposite. Turns violet to magenta in fall. Deciduous.

81 *Viburnum dentatum* Page 139

Arrow-wood

LS: Perennial shrub HT: 5 - 10 ft. BL: April - May

Flower: Flat-topped clusters to 3 in. across, white, usually long-stalked with star-shaped hairs.

Leaves: Ovate, coarsely toothed, on petioles with star-shaped hairs (also on young twigs). Deciduous.

82 *Viburnum lantanoides* (formerly *V. alnifolium*) Page 139
Witch hobble
LS: Perennial shrub HT: 6 - 10 ft. BL: April - May
Flower: Flat-topped 3 - 5 in. terminal clusters of large 5 rayed white, sterile flowers surrounding smaller ones in center.
Leaves: Dark green, wrinkled, toothed margins, opposite. Turn reddish in fall often with patches of other colors.

Viburnum rufidulum
Rusty black-haw, Southern black-haw
LS: Perennial shrub HT: 6 - 18 ft. BL: April - May
Flower: Flat-topped clusters to 5 in. across, white, individual stalks from same point, the clusters without a stalk for itself, covered with rusty hairs.
Leaves: Deciduous, elliptic, finely toothed, on short petioles with rusty hairs. Leaves shiny above, rusty hairs below.
Habitat: (all species) Woods, shady ravines.
Culture: (all species) Rich, moist soil, shade, acid.
Propagation: (all species) By stratified seed, cuttings or layering. Some varieties are slow to establish.
Note: All fruits of *Viburnum* are drupes, fleshy fruits with pits or single seeds; they are blue-black and shivel like raisins.

Horsechestnut or Buckeye Family (*Hippocastanaceae*)

Small family of deciduous or evergreen trees. Flowers red, yellow or white in terminal panicles. Calyx 5-lobed with 4 - 5 petals, 6 - 8 stamens. Leaves opposite, palmately compound.

159 *Aesculus flava* (formerly *A. octandra*) Page 158
Sweet buckeye, Yellow buckeye
LS: Perennial tree HT: 30 - 90 ft. BL: May - June
Flower: Yellow or cream colored, bell-shaped, 1 1/4 in. long, borne in oblong 6 in. clusters.
Leaves: Leaflets 5 - 7 in., ovate to oblong.

83 *Aesculus parviflora* Page 139
Bottlebrush buckeye
LS: Perennial shrub HT: 1 - 15 ft. BL: May - June
Flower: Showy, white, with long-extended stamens; many borne in a long narrow panicle resembling a "bottlebrush," sometimes to 1 ft. long.
Leaves: 5 - 7, elliptic to oblong, accuminate, nearly sessile.

235 *Aesculus pavia* Page 177

Red buckeye, Firecracker plant

LS: Perennial shrub HT: 5 - 15 ft. BL: May - June

Flower: Showy, bright red, irregular (4 unequal sized petals rolled and overlapped into a "tube"), many borne in loose panicles, 3 - 5 in. long.

Leaves: Opposite, compound, 5 elliptic leaflets with short stalks, deep green, prominent veining, arranged finger fashioned (palmate). Deciduous.

Habitat: (all species) Open woods, roadsides.

Culture: (all species) Rich moist soil, partial shade or sun.

Propagation: (all species) Sow seed when ripe in fall or stratify for 3 months. Layering.

Note: Young foliage and seed said to be poison. Blooms attract hummingbirds.

Laurel Family (*Lauraceae*)

Mostly trees and shrubs with small flowers borne in racemes or cymes, surrounded by bracts. Leaves usually evergreen, leathery, simple, aromatic.

Lindera benzoin

Spicebush

LS: Perennial shrub HT: 8 - 15 ft. BL: February - April

Flower: Very small, yellow, blooms before leaves emerge, crowded along bare stem in small, nearly stalkless clusters. Very fragrant. Scarlet fruit, often remaining after leaves fall.

Leaves: Alternate, oblong, 2 - 5 in. long, spicy fragrance.

Habitat: Woods on lower slopes and swamps.

Culture: Easy in most garden soils, partial shade, moisture.

Propagation: Division.

Note: Best planted in small clumps. Leaves turn yellow in autumn. May attract spicebush swallowtail butterflies.

Magnolia Family (*Magnoliaceae*)

Deciduous and evergreen trees and shrubs with large showy flowers and simple, alternate leaves.

Magnolia acuminata

Cucumber tree

LS: Perennial tree HT: 60 - 90 ft. BL: May - June

Flower: Cup-shaped, 6 petals 2 - 3 in. long, greenish yellow. Young fruit resembles a cucumber.

Leaves: Oval but pointed on each end, hairy beneath, deciduous, 6 - 10 in. long.

84 *Magnolia fraseri* Page 139

Fraser magnolia, Mountain magnolia

LS: Perennial tree HT: 30 - 50 ft. BL: May - June

Flower: Creamy white, fragrant, 6 - 9 petals.

Leaves: Eared at base, 6 - 9 in. long, usually grown near twig tips.

85 *Magnolia grandiflora* Page 140

Southern magnolia
LS: Perennial tree HT: 40 - 100 ft. BL: May - June
Flower: Creamy white, fragrant, 6 - 8 in. wide. Fruit - fleshy cone, bright scarlet berries.
Leaves: Shiny deep green above, rusty and hairy beneath, alternate, simple, oblong, tapering at both ends, 5 - 8 in. long, leathery and glossy, evergreen.

86 *Magnolia tripetala* Page 140

Umbrella magnolia
LS: Perennial tree HT: 20 - 40 ft. BL: May - June
Flower: Creamy white, showy, 7 - 8 in. across, cup-shaped, solitary, terminal. Fleshy seeds scarlet.
Leaves: Deciduous, large, oblong, 9 - 18 in., simple, alternate, tapered at base, grown in umbrella-like clusters.
Habitat: (all species) Woods, edges of woods, near streams.
Culture: (all species) Rich moist well-drained soil. Keep roots protected from sun and wind.
Propagation: (all species) Seeds (stratify), layering, cuttings. May be difficult to transplant.

Mallow Family (*Malvaceae*)

Made up of mainly shrubs and small trees. Leaves opposite or whorled. Flowers showy, bisexual, regular, 4 - 5 petals and sepals; 4 - 10 stamens, sometimes different lengths. Fruit a one to many seeded capsule.

236 *Hibiscus coccineus* Page 177

Scarlet rose mallow, Blazing star
LS: Perennial shrub HT: 4 - 8 ft. BL: July - October
Flower: Typically 5 petals, bright red, 4 - 7 in. across, bell-like, solitary, borne in upper leaf axils on long pedicel.
Leaves: Alternate, palmate, large, finely divided, apple green with red petioles.
Habitat: Swamps, damp areas.
Culture: Moist soil. Can grow in ordinary garden soil so long as there is ample moisture.
Propagation: Seeds. Blooms year after germination. Division.

Hibiscus militaris

Rose pink mallow, Halberd-leaved mallow
LS: Perennial shrub HT: 2 - 6 ft. BL: July - October
Flower: Five petals, rose, pink or creamy white, 3 - 5 in. across, showy, bell-shaped, borne in leaf axils.
Leaves: Dagger-like, deeply cut, 3-lobed.
Habitat: Wet areas.
Culture: Moist soil.
Propagation: Seeds sown in spring or fall.

87 *Hibiscus moscheutos* Page 140

Swamp rose mallow, Southern rose mallow
LS: Perennial shrub HT: 5 - 8 ft. BL: July - October
Flower: White or cream, rarely pink, with reddish to purple center, 4 - 8 in. across, 5 petals, solitary, borne in upper leaf axils on long pedicel, yellow stamens form tubular column, sepals surrounded by narrow bracts.
Leaves: Lanceolate to ovate, hairy beneath, up to 6 in. long, gray-green above, whitish and hairy below.
Habitat: Open swamps, marshes, wet meadows.
Culture: Average soil, at least half-day sun. Does not require excessive moisture but do not let dry out.
Propagation: Seed, division.

Olive Family (*Oleaceae*)

Deciduous or evergreen trees and shrubs. Flowers regular, 4-lobed corolla and calyx, 2 stamens, borne in modified cymes. Leaves usually opposite, simple or pinnate.

88 *Chionanthus virginicus* Page 140

Grandsir graybeard, Grancy graybeard, Fringe tree, Old Man's beard
LS: Perennial shrub HT: 5 - 20 ft. BL: May - June
Flower: Showy, small, white, 4 narrow fringe - like petals, hanging in loose, fluffy clusters 4 - 7 in. long, appear as leaves emerge. Profuse bloomer. Male and female flowers on separate plants. Blue fruit in fall.
Leaves: Simple, opposite, oblong 3 - 6 in., turn yellow in fall. Deciduous.
Habitat: Along edges of woods, fields, banks, and granite outcroppings.
Culture: Moist soil, full sun, sandy loam.
Propagation: Seed sown in the fall. Layering, cuttings. Transplants easily.

Pea Family (*Leguminosae*)

212 *Ceris canadensis* Page 171

Redbud, Judas tree
LS: Perennial shrub or tree HT: 10 - 20 ft. BL: April - May
Flower: Rosy pink, showy, pea-like, about 1/2 in. long, crowded along twigs in small clusters. Blooms appear before leaves open.
Leaves: Smooth, heart-shaped at base with pointed tip, 2 - 5 in. long, deciduous.
Habitat: Edges of woods, open woodlands, roadsides.
Culture: Semi-shade, sandy loam, alkaline soil.
Propagation: Seed or layering. Best transplanted when small.
Note: A close European relative (*Ceris siliguastrum*) is said to have been the tree upon which Judas hanged himself. The flowers blushed with shame and have been rosy purple ever since. Eastern American species (*C. canadensis*) complements dogwood and usually blooms simultaneously.

160 *Cytisus scoparius* Page 158
Scotch broom
LS: Perennial shrub HT: 2 - 8 ft. BL: March - April
Flower: Bright yellow, showy, up to 1 in. long, pea-like, calyx irregular and 2-lipped, solitary or in twos mostly at leaf axils. Very profuse. Fruit a flat pod.
Leaves: Evergreen, very small, 1/3 - 1/2 in. long, mostly trifoliate (with 3 leaflets), drop early. Stiff-branched with green, angled stems.
Habitat: Pine barrens, disturbed places.
Culture: Full sunlight, average soil (prefers sand), good drainage.
Propagation: Seed. Hard to transplant except when very small.
Note: This escape from central and southern Europe is one of the earliest shrubs to bloom. Many color forms, some with pink to red flowers, are cultivated. Similar to forsythia in its landscape uses, but grows better in poorer soils.

Rose Family (*Rosaceae*)

89 *Amelanchier laevis* Page 141
Smooth serviceberry, Allegheny serviceberry, Shadbush, Juneberry
LS: Perennial shrub or tree HT: 10 - 15 ft. BL: March - April
Flower: White, creamy or pale pink with brown sepals, 5 narrow (strap-shaped) petals, sparse drooping terminal racemes, blooms as or after leaves unfold. Purple fruits.
Leaves: Alternate, oval, heart-shaped at base, 2 - 3 in. long, bright green, bronze tinted when young. Orange in fall. Deciduous.
Habitat: Thickets, woods.
Culture: Ordinary garden soil, neutral to alkaline.
Propagation: Seed sown when ripe. Transplant suckers.
Note: Usually first native white-flowered shrub to bloom. Birds enjoy its fruits. A similar species with leaves pubescent and hairy when young is *A. arborea,* downy serviceberry, also common in Georgia.

90 *Aronia arbutifolia* Page 141
Red chokeberry
LS: Perennial shrub HT: 3 - 5 ft. BL: April - May
Flower: Small, 5 rounded petals, white with black anthers, in terminal clusters. Fruit bright red, pea-sized, remains colorful almost all winter.
Leaves: Oblong, pointed on both ends, simple, alternate, toothed, 2 in. long, green above, gray and hairy beneath; distinguished from other small shrubs by black glands along midvein beneath. Turn red in fall. Deciduous.
Habitat: Hillsides, slopes.
Culture: Ordinary garden soil, full sun, moist.
Propagation: Seeds, cuttings, layering.
Note: Often forms dense colonies with masses of red fruits, showy.

213 *Malus angustifolia* Page 172
Southern wild crabapple
LS: Perennial tree HT: 5 - 25 ft. BL: March - May
Flower: 1 in. across with 5 petals, 5 sepals, shell pink (fading to white) in umbel-like clusters, numerous stamens. Very showy, fragrant. Appear before foliage. Fruit—pome

(apple-like), fleshy, 1 in. in diameter, sour, yellow green.
Leaves: Oblong, usually toothed, dark green, lighter underneath, alternate, 1 - 2 in. long, deciduous. Branches thorny.
Habitat: Open woodlands, fields.
Culture: Deep, fairly rich, well-drained soil, slightly alkaline.
Propagation: Seed. Deep rooted. Hard to transplant except when extremely small.

Saxifrage Family (*Saxifragaceae*)

91 *Hydrangea arborescens* Page 141
Wild hydrangea, Sevenbark
LS: Perennial shrub HT: 3 - 5 ft. BL: June - August
Flower: Small, white to cream, fertile florets surrounded by sterile flowers, in dense flat-topped or slightly rounded clusters 2 - 4 in. wide.
Leaves: Pale green, simple, opposite, oval, sharply toothed, 3 - 4 in. long, deciduous.

92 *Hydrangea quercifolia* Page 141
Oakleaf hydrangea
LS: Perennial shrub HT: 4 - 6 ft. BL: June - August
Flower: Pure white, fading lavender-pink, 1 - 2 in. in diameter, forming a pyramidal cluster 4 - 8 in. long, showy; outer flowers sterile.
Leaves: 3 - 7, deeply lobed (resembling red oak leaves), opposite, hairy beneath, deep green, felty and white beneath, turn wine in fall. Limbs crooked with brownish shreddy bark. Deciduous.
Habitat: (both species) Along streams, rocky slopes, open woods.
Culture: (both species) Rich moist soil, shade, slightly acid (blooms more freely in semi-shade).
Propagation: (both species) Cuttings, division.
Note: *Hydrangea* is sometimes confused with *Viburnum*. Major differences between these two commonly cultivated kinds of shrubs include fruit and flower characteristics. The fruit of Viburnum is fleshy, one-seeded, brightly colored or raisin-like, whereas the fruit of Hydrangea is dry, brownish with many seeds. *Viburnum* flowers have 5 stamens, *Hydrangea* flowers have 10 stamens.

93 *Itea virginica* Page 142
Virginia sweetspire, Virginia willow, Tassel-white
LS: Perennial shrub HT: 4 - 8 ft. BL: April - June
Flower: White, small, 5 narrow petals, 5 persistent sepals, borne in showy upright terminal racemes, 2 1/2 - 5 in. long, fragrant.
Leaves: Finely toothed, oval, 2 - 4 in. long, alternate, fall color a spectacular crimson, deciduous.
Habitat: Wet boggy areas, swamps, edges of streams.
Culture: Moist, well-drained, fertile soil, acidic, full sun to light shade.
Propagation: Cuttings taken in June, root division, seeds.

94 *Philadelphus inodorus* Page 142
Mock orange, English dogwood
LS: Perennial shrub HT: 4 - 8 ft. BL: April - May

Flower: White, 4 petals, 1 - 3 in a cluster, cuplike, 1 - 2 in. wide, numerous yellow stamens.
Leaves: Opposite, oval, long pointed, smooth, 2 - 4 in. long, bark papery and peeling, arching branches. Deciduous.
Habitat: Fields, pastures, edges of woods.
Culture: Ordinary soil, sun or semi-shade.
Propagation: Seed, cuttings, layering, division.

Stafftree Family (*Celastraceae*)

Evergreen or deciduous shrubs, trees or vines. Flower light green, small, 4 - 5 petals, sepals and stamens inconspicuous, borne in cymes or panicles. Fruit a drupe, capsule or berry, often brightly colored aril exposed in the autumn. Leaves opposite, alternate or whorled, simple.

Euonymus altropurpurea
Burning bush, Wahoo
LS: Perennial shrub HT: 6 - 12 ft. BL: April
Flower: Small, purplish. Crimson, smooth, 4-lobed capsule bursts open in fall revealing seeds enclosed in scarlet coverings.
Leaves: Deciduous, opposite, elliptic, hairy below, turn brilliant red in fall, 4 angled branches.

237 *Euonymus americana* Page 178
Heart's-a-bustin', Strawberry bush
LS: Perennial shrub HT: 2 - 8 ft. BL: April - May
Flower: Early flowers very tiny and inconspicuous. Grow in small clusters in leaf axils. Seed pod enlarges throughout the summer. Red-lavender, warty, usually 5-lobed seed capsule bursts open in fall revealing 4 - 6 bright, glossy orange-red seeds.
Leaves: Bright green, opposite, 1 1/2 - 3 in. long, oblong, green or gray twigs. Deciduous. Sparsely branched.

Euonymus obovata
Trailing wahoo, Running strawberry bush
LS: Perennial shrub HT: 1 - 3 ft. BL: April - May
Flower: Same as *E. americana*. Fruits are similar but 3 - 5 lobed.
Leaves: Same, except trailing habit. Sometimes a variegated leaf form is available.
Habitat: (all species) Rich woods, near streams.
Culture: (all species) Shade or semi-shade, rich soil.
Propagation: (all species) Seed—stratify and sow in the spring. Cuttings taken from old wood. Division.

Storax Family (*Styraceae*)

Trees and shrubs. Flowers regular, calyx 4 - 5 lobed with 4 - 8 petals, joined at base, many stamens. Leaves alternate and simple.

95 *Halesia carolina* Page 142

Silverbell, Snowdrop

LS: Perennial tree HT: 40 ft. BL: May - June

Flower: Small to 3/4 in. long, white, bell-shaped, drooping from branches in small clusters. Blooms profusely.

Leaves: Oblong, 2 - 4 in. long, blunt, toothed, alternate, deciduous. Spreading branches.

Habitat: Open woods, edges of woods.

Culture: Rich loamy soil, well drained, sheltered from the wind.

Propagation: Seed stratified and sown in the fall. Layering, root cuttings.

Vervain Family (*Verbenaceae*)

287 *Callicarpa americana* Page 190

American beauty bush, French mulberry, Beauty berry

LS: Perennial shrub HT: 4 - 5 ft. BL: June - July

Flower: Small, tubular, bluish, in dense short-stalked clusters in leaf axils. Fruit berrylike and in leaf axils, showy, profuse, green turning magenta or violet in fall. Forms with white berries sometimes seen.

Leaves: Simple, opposite, blunt toothed, tapering to a point, 3 - 6 in., browning below. Deciduous.

Habitat: Woods, thickets, roadsides, granite outcroppings.

Culture: Rich moist soil, sun or partial shade.

Propagation: Cuttings, layering. Seed—plants grown from seed flower the second year.

Note: Grown more for berries than for flowers. May be somewhat aggressive.

Willow Family (*Salicaceae*)

Deciduous shrubs and trees. Flowers are borne in silky hairy catkins, male and female flowers borne on separate plants. Leaves alternate, simple, deciduous.

319 *Salix discolor* Page 198

Pussy willow

LS: Perennial shrub HT: 5 - 15 ft. BL: February - April

Flower: Silvery with brownish-yellow undertones, catkin (female flower) without petals or sepals, covered in silky hairs (fuzzy), alternate, along stem in axil of bracts. Blooms before leaves unfold.

Leaves: Elliptic, 2 - 3 in. long, blue-green beneath, toothed towards tip, alternate. Deciduous.

Habitat: Stream banks, damp areas.

Culture: Damp soil, loamy, sun or light shade. Root system extensive.

Propagation: Seed sown as soon as ripe. Cuttings rooted in moist soil.

Note: Male and female flowers are borne on separate plants. *Salix babylonica* (weeping willow) is a common cultivated tree.

Witch-Hazel Family (*Hamamelidaceae*)

Deciduous and evergreen trees and shrubs. Flowers borne in heads or racemes, 4 - 5 sepals, 4 - 5 petals or none, 4 or more stamens. Leaves alternate, simple, sometimes palmately lobed.

96 *Fothergilla gardenii* Page 142
Dwarf witch alder
LS: Perennial shrub HT: 3 - 5 ft. BL: March - April
Flower: White, no petals, profuse protruding and showy stamens, borne in terminal clusters, 2 - 3 in. long, bloom before or as leaves unfold.
Leaves: Alternate, toothed, coarse, oval, 1 - 3 in. long, deciduous, turn brilliant yellow to scarlet in fall.
Habitat: Cool, damp woods.
Culture: Acid, loamy soil, moist, half shade. Protect from wind.
Propagation: Seed, layering (will not root for 2 years), suckers and root cuttings.
Note: Threatened species. Habitat threatened with logging of hardwoods and wetlands destruction. Attractive early bloomer and fall foliage; best in small clumps.

161 *Hamamelis virginica* Page 159
Witch hazel, Snapping alder
LS: Perennial shrub HT: 8 - 15 ft. BL: October - January
Flower: Four elongated strap-shaped petals, spidery, delicate, bright yellow, 3/4 in. wide.
Leaves: Alternate, simple, elliptic, wavy-toothed, coarse, 4 - 6 in. Turn soft yellow in fall. Deciduous.
Habitat: Woods, along streams.
Culture: Cool, damp, ordinary soil.
Propagation: Layering. Seed germination takes 2 years.
Note: Good food for the birds. The only woody native plant that starts blooming in the fall and winter.

VINES

Bignonia Family (*Bignoniaceae*)

Trees, shrubs or vines with showy, tubular or trumpetlike 5 parted calyx, 5 parted corolla, 5 stamens. Leaves opposite, simple or compound.

162 *Bignonia capreolata* Page 159
Cross vine, Trumpet flower
LS: Perennial HT: 30 - 50 ft. BL: April - June
Flower: Reddish yellow outside, yellow-orange within, about 2 in. long, trumpet shaped, borne in clusters from leaf axils. Resembles trumpet creeper but corolla is shorter and petals more flaring.
Leaves: Evergreen, dark green, bronzy on back, narrowly heart shaped, stiff, opposite, compound with 2 stalked 2 in. long leaflets. Climbs by branched tendrils that emerge from leaf axils.

Habitat: Woods, swamps, along streams.
Culture: Rich moist soil, warm (sensitive to cold). Prune hard after flowering to control height.
Propagation: Cuttings of half-ripened wood. Layering. Division.
Note: Cross section of stem (pith) reveals a cross. Attracts hummingbirds.

174 *Campsis radicans* Page 162
Trumpet creeper, Trumpet vine
LS: Perennial HT: 30 ft. BL: July - September
Flower: Brilliant red-orange corolla, trumpet shaped, 3 - 5 in. long, fleshy texture, borne in terminal or axil clusters.
Leaves: Compound, made up of 12 toothed leaflets, opposite and elliptic, deciduous. Climbs by aerial rootlets.
Habitat: Moist woods, roadsides, open places.
Culture: Rich soil, full or partial sun.
Propagation: Division or seed. Tends to be aggressive. Can be kept pruned and bushlike by cutting back laterals and supporting with a stake.
Note: Attracts hummingbirds.

Birthwort Family (*Aristolochiaceae*)

320 *Aristolochia durior* (formerly *macrophylla*) Page 198
Dutchman's pipe, Pipevine
LS: Perennial HT: 30 ft. BL: April - June
Flower: Solitary, calyx corolla-like, tubular, usually pipe or U-shaped, brownish-purple.
Leaves: Heart shaped or cordate, alternate, 6 - 14 in. wide, stalked, deciduous, climbing habit.
Habitat: Moist woods, stream banks, high altitudes.
Culture: Moist soil.
Propagation: Seeds, cuttings of ripened wood, layering.

Buttercup Family (*Ranunculaceae*)

97 *Clematis virginiana* Page 143
Virgin's bower, Satin curls, Love vine
LS: Perennial HT: 20 ft. BL: July - September
Flower: Flat-topped flower clusters with lacy, creamy white flowers consisting of 4 petal-like sepals, to 1 in. wide, numerous stamens. Borne in dense panicles in leaf axils. Profuse bloomer. Fragrant. Feathery fruits (single-seeded, dry, with long hairy style branch).
Leaves: Thin, opposite, ovate. Compound (3 sharply toothed leaflets), prominent veins, 2 1/2 - 3 in. long. Deciduous. Climb by means of stems and tough twisting leaf petioles.
Habitat: Roadsides, edge of woods, moist places.
Culture: Shade or sun, moist, loam, somewhat alkaline soil.
Propagation: Seed or division.
Note: Male and female flowers on separate plants. There are many other native and introduced species of Clematis worthy of cultivation.

Dogbane Family (*Apocynaceae*)

288 *Vinca minor* Page 190

Periwinkle, Myrtle

LS: Perennial HT: 6 - 8 in. BL: March - June

Flower: Blue violet or lavender with white star in center, 5 lobed, funnel-shaped corolla, up to 1 in. across, borne singly in leaf axils.

Leaves: Lush dark glossy green, ovate, evergreen, opposite, 1 1/2 in. long.

Habitat: Woodland borders, roadsides, shaded areas, under trees.

Culture: Rich or ordinary soil, shade or partial shade.

Propagation: Cuttings. Seed.

Note: An escape from Europe. Ideal groundcover. Spreads rapidly. *Vinca major*, greater periwinkle, is similar with larger, more ovate leaves and larger flowers to 2 in. across.

Morning Glory Family (*Convolvulaceae*)

Vines with 5 united petals which flare into bell-shaped showy blossoms.

238 *Ipomoea coccinea* (sometimes called *Quamoclit coccinea*) Page 178

Scarlet starglory, Star ipomoea, Hummingbird plant, Red Morning Glory

LS: Annual HT: 3 - 9 ft. BL: July - October

Flower: Corolla scarlet with yellow throat, tubular, about 3/4 in. across, 5 united petals, 5 sepals, 1 1/2 in. long, borne singly in leaf axils.

Leaves: Ovate to heart-shaped, 1 1/2 -4 in. long, alternate, twining habit.

Habitat: Fields, roadsides, waste places.

Culture: Ordinary soil, sun.

Propagation: Seeds.

Note: An escape from Mexico.

Honeysuckle Family (*Caprifoliaceae*)

239 *Lonicera sempervirens* Page 178

Coral honeysuckle, Woodbine, Red trumpet honeysuckle

LS: Perennial HT: 15 ft. BL: April - August

Flower: Slender, tubular, 1 - 2 in. long, deep red outside, yellowish inside, showy, borne in whorled terminal clusters. Red berries.

Leaves: Deep blue-green, pale beneath, opposite, ovate, upper 1 or 2 pairs perfoliate, evergreen. Twining habit.

Habitat: Woods, swamps, thickets, along streams.

Culture: Full or partial sun, average soil.

Propagation: Seeds or cuttings.

Note: Attracts hummingbirds.

Logania Family (*Loganiaceae*)

163 *Gelsemium sempervirens* Page 159

Carolina jessamine

LS: Perennial HT: 10 - 20 ft. BL: March - May

Flower: Tubular, bright yellow, 5 lobed, flaring mouth, about 1 in. across, very fragrant. Borne in dense clusters from leaf axils.

Leaves: Evergreen, glossy green, opposite, oblong with pointed tips, 1 - 2 1/2 in. long.

Habitat: Thickets, woods, sandy areas, roadsides.

Culture: Sun or partial shade, rich garden loam.

Propagation: Cuttings or seed. Spreads by suckers. Transplant.

Passion Flower Family (*Passifloraceae*)

Vines, trees, shrubs and herbs, may have showy flowers and edible fruit. Flowers have 5 sepals, 5 petals, fringed center. Alternate leaves.

289 *Passiflora incarnata* Page 191

Passion flower, Maypop

LS: Perennial HT: 10 ft. BL: June - September

Flower: Pale lavender, borne in leaf axils, 5 sepals, 5 petals, fringed on crown, 5 stamen, 3 stigma, 3 styles. Up to 3 in. in diameter. Fragrant. Fleshy fruit yellow when ripe (edible).

Leaves: Palmately lobed, 3 - 5 in. wide, alternate, stalked. Deciduous. Climbs via tendrils opposite the leaves.

Habitat: Dry areas, fields, roadsides, sandy thickets.

Culture: Full sun, average soil. Good drainage.

Propagation: Seed.

Note: Flower is said to have reminded the early missionaries of the crucifixion, accounting for its botanical and common names.

Pea Family (*Leguminosae*)

290 *Clitoria mariana* Page 191

Butterfly pea, Pigeon wing

LS: Perennial HT: 1 - 3 ft. BL: July - August

Flower: Lavender-blue, up to 2 in., borne singly in leaf axils, pea-shaped (broad standard petals, keel and small spur at base).

Leaves: Compound, 3 entire leaflets, alternate, lanceolate. Climbs via tendrils.

Habitat: Dry places, thin woods, open fields.

Culture: Acid soil.

Propagation: Seed. Transplant.

214 *Lathyrus latifolius* Page 172

Everlasting pea

LS: Perennial HT: 1 - 5 ft. BL: May - September

Flower: Purple, pink or white, sweetpea like (one upstanding, two lateral and two lower petals), stipules two lobed, borne in short stalked axillary racemes. No fragrance.

Leaves: Alternate, compound (a pair of blades 2 - 4 in. long) with terminal tendrils. Flat-winged stems.
Habitat: Roadsides, open fields.
Culture: Good garden soil, moisture.
Propagation: Seed.
Note: Native of Europe, widely planted and naturalized.

215 *Schrankia microphylla* Page 172
Sensitive briar
LS: Perennial HT: 2 - 3 ft. BL: June - September
Flower: Deep pink, fluffy rounded heads 1 in. in diameter, borne in leaf axils.
Leaves: Alternate, twice pinnately divided into numerous narrow opposite leaflets, close when touched, thorny. Branching, trailing habit.
Habitat: Hillsides, fields, dry woods.
Culture: Ordinary soil. Thorns make difficult to handle.
Propagation: Seed.

291 *Wisteria frutescens* Page 191
American wisteria
LS: Perennial HT: 20 - 40 ft. BL: May - June
Flower: Lavender or purple, pea-like, 1/2 in. long, in drooping tight racemes usually less than 5 in. long. Blooms after leaves appear.
Leaves: Alternate, toothless, compound, 9 - 15 elliptic leaflets, 1 - 2 in. long, arranged feather fashioned with odd one at end. Deciduous.
Habitat: Stream banks, woodsides, swamps.
Culture: Rich garden loam, partial sun, moisture.
Propagation: Cuttings. Seed (scarify before planting). Long fibrous root system. Transplant only when small.

292 *Wisteria macrostachya* Page 191
Kentucky wisteria
LS: Perennial HT: 10 - 40 ft. BL: May
Flower: Pea-like, borne in drooping clusters, 5 - 8 in. long, lavender or lilac with a yellow spot.
Leaves: 9 - 15 alternate leaflets, long pointed, elliptic, feather-fashioned, compound, toothless, very profuse.
Habitat: Thin woods, edges of woods.
Culture: Ordinary soil.
Propagation: Seed. Division of small plants.
Note: Climb via twining stems. Prune back straggly growth to control height. Less aggressive than Japanese wisteria (*W. floribunda*) or Chinese wisteria (*W. sinensis*). The introduced species tend to smother trees, almost like kudzu. They have velvety pods, and their flowers lack yellow spots. The native wisteria have smooth pods and lilac flowers with yellow spots.

Rose Family (*Rosaceae*)

216 *Rosa carolina* Page 172

Carolina rose, Pasture rose

LS: Perennial HT: 1 - 3 ft. BL: June - July

Flower: Pale pink, 1 1/2 - 2 in. across, delicate, numerous yellow stamens.

Leaves: Dull green, pinnately divided into 5 - 9 segments. Straight prickles.

Habitat: Sandy or rocky fields, open woods.

Culture: Full sun or light shade.

Propagation: Transplants easily. Be sure to get enough of the creeping root.

98 *Rosa laevigata* Page 143

Cherokee rose

LS: Perennial HT: 30 ft. BL: April - May

Flower: Single, 2 - 3 in. across, pure white, yellow stamens.

Leaves: Evergreen and glossy with 3 leaflets, high climbing, sharp recurved prickles.

Habitat: Along roadsides, fields.

Culture: Full sun, average garden soil.

Propagation: Cuttings, division.

Note: State flower of Georgia. An escape from China.

99 *Rosa multiflora* Page 143

Multiflora rose

LS: Perennial HT: 10 ft. BL: May - June

Flower: Small, less than one inch (3/4 in. wide), white, form clusters, 5 petals, 5 sepals, stamens and pistils numerous.

Leaves: Pinnately divided into 7 - 9 toothed leaflets about 1 in. long, prickly, arching stem recurved.

Habitat: Fields, roadsides, edges of woods.

Culture: Sun or semi-shade, ordinary garden soil.

Propagation: Division. Cuttings. Transplant.

Note: This shrubby climbing vine is commonly used as a hedge, but may become aggressive; another Chinese introduction widely escaped (spread by birds).

Stafftree Family (*Celastraceae*)

164 *Celastrus scandens* Page 159

Bittersweet (American), Waxwork

LS: Perennial HT: 7 - 20 ft. BL: April - June

Flower: Very small, greenish yellow, inconspicuous, in terminal clusters. Fruit yellowish capsule splits when ripe, revealing clusters of brilliant orange-red seed.

Leaves: Alternate, simple, oblong, wavy toothed, petioled, 2 in. long, deciduous.

Habitat: Woods, fence rows, roadsides.

Culture: Ordinary garden soil, sun or shade.

Propagation: Seed sown in the fall. Stem or root cuttings or by suckers.

Note: Male and female flowers sometimes on separate plants which causes non-fruiting. Rampant grower. Prune to control. In danger of extinction in some areas. Attracts birds; fruit clusters useful in dried flower arrangements.

1. Spider Lily p.23

2. Magic Lily p.24

3. Twinleaf p.25

4. Mayapple p.25

5. Bluets p.26

6. Partridge Berry p.26

7. Dutchman's Breeches p.28

8. Squirrel Corn p.28

9. Cancer-Root p.30

10. Doll's Eyes (Bloom) p.31

11. Doll's Eyes (Seed) p.31

12. Thimbleweed p.31

13. Rue Anemone p.32

14. Sharp-lobed Hepatica p.32

15. Golden Seal p.32

16. Tall Meadow-rue p.33

17/177. Yarrow p.35

18. Field Pussytoes p.35

19. Ox-eye Daisy p.36

20. Daisy Fleabane p.39

21. Snakeroot p.39

22. Sweet Everlasting p.40

23. Wild Quinine p.42

24. Silver-rod p.44

25. Galax p.47

26. Oconee Bells p.48

27. Pale Gentian p.49

28. Fly Poison p.54

29. Fairy Wand p.55

30. Lily of the Valley p.55

31. Wild Lily of the Valley p.56

32. False Lily of the Valley p.58

33. Star-of-Bethlehem p.58

34. Solomon's Seal p.59

35. False Solomon's Seal p.59

36/221. Wakerobin p.59

37. Large Flowered Trillium p.60

38. Southern Nodding Trillium p.60

39. Painted Trillium p.60

40. Bear Grass p.61

41. Horse-balm p.64

42. Mountain Mint p.65

43. Mistletoe p.67

44. Toothwort p.67

45/190. Ladyslipper p.68

46. Rattlesnake Orchid p.69

47. Nodding Ladie's Tresses p.70

48. Slender Ladie's Tresses p.70

49. Queen Anne's Lace p.71

50. Wild Indigo p.71

51. Evening Lychnis p.73

52. Bloodroot p.77

53. Shooting Star p.78

54. Goat's Beard p.79

55. False Goat's Beard p.80

56. Bishop's Cap p.80

57. Foamflower p.80

58. White Turtlehead p.82

59. Flowering Spurge p.86

60. Snow-on-the-Mountain p.86

61. Sweet White Violet p.89

62. Canada Violet p.89

63/283. Butterfly Violet p.90

64. Sweet Water Lily p.91

65. Striped Pipissewa p.91

66. New Jersey Tea p.96

67. Flowering Dogwood p.97

68. Stiff Dogwood p.98

69. Coastal Sweetbells p.98

70. Dog Hobble p.98

71. Stagger Bush p.99

72. Sourwood p.99

73. Mountain Fetterbush p.99

74. Sparkleberry p.99

75. Highbush Blueberry p.100

76. Alabama Azalea p.101

77. Sweet Azalea p.101

78. White Swamp Azalea p.103

79. Great Laurel p.103

80. Mapleleaf Virburnum p.104

81. Arrow-wood p.104

82. Witch Hobble p.105

83. Bottlebrush Buckeye p.105

84. Fraser Magnolia p.106

85. Southern Magnolia p.107

86. Umbrella Magnolia p.107

87. Swamp Rose Mallow p.108

88. Grancy Graybeard p.108

89. Shadbush p.109

90. Chokeberry p.109

91. Wild Hydrangea p.110

92. Oakleaf Hydrangea p.110

93. Virginia Sweetspire p.110

94. English Dogwood p.110

95. Silverbell p.112

96. Dwarf Witch Alder p.113

97. Virgin's Bower p.114

98. Cherokee Rose p.118

99. Multiflora Rose p.118

100. Star Grass p.24

101. Golden Club p.25

102. Squaw Root p.30

103. Bulbous Buttercup p.33

104. Creeping Buttercup p.33

105. Prickly Pear p.34

106. Tickseed Sunflower p.36

107. Green and Gold p.37

108. Maryland Golden Aster p.37

109. Lanceleaf Coreopsis p.37

110. Tall Coreopsis p.38

111. Hairy Sunflower p.41

112. Narrow-leaved Sunflower p.41

113. Woodland Sunflower p.41

114. Stiff Sunflower p.41

115. Jerusalem Artichoke p.41

116. Black-eyed Susan p.43

117. Green-headed Coneflower p.43

118. Bear's Paw p.43

119. Southern Ragwort p.43

120. Blue Stemmed Goldenrod p.44

121. Canada Goldenrod p.45

122. Erect Goldenrod p.45

123. Late Goldenrod p.45

124. Lance-leaf Goldenrod p.45

125. Gray Goldenrod p.45

126. Sweet Goldenrod p.45

127. Hard-leafed Goldenrod p.46

128. Elm-leafed Goldenrod p.46

129. Tansy p.47

130. Stone Mountain Yellow Daisy p.47

131. Evening Primrose p.51

132. Sundrops p.51

133. Four O'Clock p.52

134. Yellow Iris p.53

135. Trout Lily p.56

136. Canada Lily p.56

137. Indian Cucumber Root p.58

138. Yellow Trillium p.60

139. Big Merrybells p.60

140. Woods Merrybells p.61

141. Merrybells p.61

142. Clammy Ground Cherry p.68

143. Yellow Ladyslipper (large) p.69

144. Yellow Ladyslipper (small) p.69

145. Yellow Indigo p.71

146. Golden Trumpets p.76

147. Hooded Pitcher Plant p.76

148. Celadine Poppy p.77

149. Fringed Loosestrife p.78

150. Whorled Loosestrife p.78

151. Dwarf Cinquefoil p.79

152. Fern-leaved Foxglove p.82

153. Butter-and-Eggs p.83

154. Mullein p.84

155. Pale Touch-Me-Not p.87

156. Spear-leaved Violet p.89

157. Downy Yellow Violet p.90

158. Pinesap p.91

159. Yellow Buckeye p.105

160. Scotchbroom p.109

161. Witch Hazel p.113

162. Cross Vine p.113

163. Carolina Jessamine p.116

164. Bittersweet p.118

165. Blackberry Lily p.53

166. Tawny Day Lily p.56

167. Tiger Lily p.57

168. Wood Lily p.57

169. Turk's Cap Lily p.57

170. Butterfly Weed p.62

171. Yellow Fringed Orchid p.69

172. Spotted Touch Me Not p.87

173. Florida Azalea p.101

174. Trumpet Creeper p.114

175. Fringed Bleeding Heart p.28

176. Round-Lobed Hepatica p.32

177/17. Yarrow p.35

178. Cosmos p.38

179. Purple Coneflower p.38

180. Spreading Dogbane p.48

181. Rose Pink p.49

182. Trailing Arbutus p.50

183. Showy Evening Primrose p.51

184. Catesby's Trillium p.59

185. Virginia Meadow-Beauty p.62

186. Blunt-Leaved Milkweed p.62

187. Racemed Milkwort p.63

188. Lemon Mint p.64

189. Dame's Rocket p.67

190/45. Pink Ladyslipper p.68

191 Showy Orchis p.70

192. Summer Phlox p.72

193. Thrift p.73

194. Deptford Pink p.73

195. Maiden Pink p.73

196. Mullein Pink p.74

197. Bouncing Bet p.74

198. Fringed Campion p.75

199. Narrowleaf Spring Beauty p.78

200. Turtlehead p.82

201. Foxglove Beardtongue p.83

202. Hairy Beardtongue p.84

203. Live Forever p.85

204. Rose Verbena p.88

205. Common Wood Sorrel p.92

206. Mountain Laurel p.98

207. Piedmont Azalea p.102

208. Oconee Azalea p.102

209. Pinxter Flower p.102

210. Pink-Shell Azalea p.102

211. Piedmont Rhododendron p.103

212. Redbud p.108

213. Southern Wildcrabapple p.109

214. Everlasting Pea p.116

215. Sensitive Briar p.117

216. Carolina Rose p.118

217. Cardinal Flower p.29

218. Columbine p.31

219. Indian Blanket p.40

220. Whipperwill Flower p.59

221/36. Wakerobin p.59

222. Vasey's Trillium p.60

223. Indian Pink p.61

224. Bee Balm p.64

225. Scarlet Sage p.66

226. Standing Cypress p.72

227. Fire Pink p.75

228. Indian Paint Brush p.82

229. Wood Betony p.83

230. Wild Poinsettia p.86

231. Sweet Shrub p.97

232. Flame Azalea p.101

233. Plumleaf Azalea p.102

234. American Holly (Berry) p.104

235. Red Buckeye p.106

236. Blazing Star p.107

237. Heart's-a-Bustin' p.111

238. Hummingbird Plant p.115

239. Red Trumpet Honeysuckle p.115

240. Wild Petunia p.23

241 Bluets p.26

242. Violet Butterwort p.27

243. Southern Harebell p.29

244. Indian Tabacco p.29

245. Downy Lobelia p.29

246. Venus Looking Glass p.30

247. New England Purple Aster p.35

248. Bachelor's Button p.36

249. Wild Ageratum p.38

250. Purple Coneflower p.39

251. Elephant Foot p.39

252. Hollow Joe Pye Weed p.39

253. Sweet Joe Pye Weed p.40

254. Large Blazing Star p.42

255. Dense Blazing Star p.42

256. Blazing Star p.42

257. Stoke's Aster p.46

258. New York Ironweed p.47

259. Stiff Gentian p.49

260. Soapwort Gentian p.49

261. Wild Geranium p.50

262. Crested Drawf Iris p.53

263. Vernal Iris p.53

264. Blue Flag p.54

265. Wild Hyacinth p.54

266. Grape Hyacinth p.58

267. Curtiss Milkwort p.63

268. False Dragonhead p.65

269. Heal-All p.65

270. Hairy Skullcap p.66

271. Large-flowered Skullcap p.66

272. Wild Lupine p.71

273. Wild Sweet William p.72

274. Gerardia p.81

275. Trinity p.84

276. Spiderwort p.84

277. Stiff Verbena p.88

278. Moss Verbena p.88

279. Dog Violet p.89

280. Southern Wood Violet p.89

281. Birdfoot Violet p.89

282. Johnny Jump Up p.90

283/63. Common Blue Violet p.90

284. Scorpion Weed p.90

285. Violet Wood Sorrel p.92

286. Mountain Rosebay p.103

287. Beauty Berry p.112

288. Periwinkle p.115

289. Passion Flower p.116

290. Butterfly Pea p.116

291. American Wisteria p.117

292. Kentucky Wisteria p.117

293. Bluets p.26

294. Great Lobelia p.30

295. Chicory p.37

296. Virginia Bluebells p.52

297. Blue-eyed Grass p.54

298. Bugle p.63

299. Dayflower p.85

300. Green Dragon p.24

301. Jack-in-the-Pulpit p.24

302. Adder's Mouth p.69

303. Ground-Cedar p.93

304. Common Horsetail p.93

305. Cinnamon Fern p.93

306. Royal Fern p.94

307. Maidenhair Fern p.94

308. Ebony Spleenwort Fern p.94

309. Southern Lady Fern p.94

310. Sensitive Fern p.95

311. Christmas Fern p.95

312. Bracken Fern p.95

313. Broad Beech Fern p.95

314. New York Fern p.96

315. Heart Leaf p.27

316. Wild Ginger p.27

317. Narrow Leafed Cat-tail p.34

318. Broad Leafed Cat-tail p.34

319. Pussy Willow p.112

320. Dutchman's Pipe p.114

A WILDFLOWER LOVE LETTER

Dear BOUNCING BET,

Oh, my PASSION FLOWER, my HEART'S-A-BUSTIN' for you, and it MAYPOP. Time spent away from you is BITTERSWEET. There is NONE SO PRETTY as you and your BABY BLUE EYES.

You can HEAL ALL of my BLEEDING HEART by saying you'll FORGET ME NOT and be my QUEEN OF THE MEADOW. We'll be married at ST. ANDREW'S CROSS by JACK IN THE PULPIT in his BISHOP'S CAP. It will be a PENNYROYAL wedding highlighted with FAIRY WANDS and GOLDENRODS. The MERRY BELLS will ring and the TRUMPETS will sound. We'll decorate the church in GREEN AND GOLD. BLACK-EYED SUSAN, PRIMROSE and BLUE-EYED MARY can be your attendants. You might get SWEET CICELY if you ASTER. They'll be pretty in PINK. I'll use SWEET WILLIAM, STINKING BENJAMIN and PERIWINKLE.

So, comb your LADIE'S TRESSES until they look like SATIN CURLS. Put on your LADY SLIPPERS. Fasten your BLUE BONNET and ORANGE PLUME with HATPINS. Take a final glimpse in VENUS' LOOKING GLASS, hitch your DAME'S ROCKET to a SHOOTING STAR and be here before the SUNDROPS.

Be sure to bring QUEEN ANNE'S LACE and ADAM'S NEEDLE to make your wedding dress. You'll need FAIRY CAPS and GOLDTHREAD for your veil. Don't forget the FOXGLOVE for you FIVE FINGERS. I'll be decked out in my best DUTCHMAN'S BREECHES and HOODED SKULLCAP.

I'm ready to abandon my BACHELOR BUTTONS. Unless you TREAD SOFTLY I'll be a BLUE SAILOR and waste away until I have an OLD MAN'S BEARD. If you say yes, then I'll STICK TIGHT to you and be your

SWEET EVERLASTING
JOHNNY JUMP UP

Betty Benson
September, 1987

GLOSSARY

ALTERNATE - A leaf arrangement in which a single leaf emerges from a stem at one point. Not opposite or whorled.

ANNUAL - A plant that completes its life cycle from seed germination to seed production in one year. It depends on the dissemination and germination of its seed to continue its existence into another year.

AXIL - The angle where the leaf joins the main stem.

AXILLARY - Applies to organs that grow in the axil, i.e., buds, flowers, etc.

BASAL - Leaves positioned at the base of a stem.

BIENNIAL - A plant with a two year life cycle. It produces leaves the first year, flowers the second year, then dies.

BIPINNATE - A compound leaf with leaflets divided into secondary leaflets.

BLADE - The thin, flattened, expanded part of a leaf or petal.

BRACT - A modified leaf close to a flower, sometimes unlike other foliage in size, shape and/or color.

CALYX - The leaflike outer sepals of a flower, usually green.

CAULINE - Belonging to or growing on the stem.

CLEFT - Cut halfway in from the margin.

COMPOSITE - A central cluster of disc florets surrounded by ray florets, as in ox-eye daisy.

COMPOUND - Leaf with 2 or more separate and smaller leaflets.

CORDATE - Heart-shaped with pointed tip.

COROLLA - The complete circle of petals of a flower, usually colored and showy. Petals may be separated or united.

CORYMB - A short and flat-topped or rounded cluster with the outer pedicels longer and the outer flowers opening first.

CRENATE - Round-toothed along the margins.

CYATHIUM - Inflorescence of Euphorbia—cuplike involucre bearing flowers from its base.

CYME - A broad or flat cluster of blooms in which the center flower opens first.

DELTOID - Triangular (broad at base, pointed at apex).

DISC (DISK) - Tiny regular or tubular flowers (florets) that make up the center part of a composite flower head.

DISSECTED - Deeply cut into numerous segments.

ELLIPTIC - Oblong with ends equally rounded.

ENDANGERED SPECIES - A species in danger of extinction thoughout all or part of its range or one legally designated endangered by Endangered Species Act.

ENTIRE LEAF - A leaf margin without teeth (not cut, divided or lobed in any way).

FALL - The lower petal of an iris.

FEATHER VEINED - Small thin veins which extend from the center vein similar to the barbs of a feather.

FLORET - A small individual flower (petal) in composite flowers.

FROND - The leaf of a fern.

HEAD - A crowded cluster of flowers without a stalk, being attached directly to the stem.

HERBACEOUS - A plant that does not survive above the ground over the winter, non-woody.

INFLORESCENCE - The arrangement of more than one flower on a stem, the flower cluster.

INTERNODE - That portion of a stem between one node and the next.

INVOLUCRE - A whorl or spiral of bracts beneath or around a flower or inflorescence.

IRREGULAR FLOWER - One which is not radially symmetrical—petals and/or sepals not uniform in shape.

KEEL - The ridge on the back of many petals and some leaves OR the two lower and united petals in the pea flower.

LANCEOLATE - Lance shaped, longer than wide and widest below the middle.

LATERAL - Inflorescence borne other than on tip or terminal end of stem.

LAYER - A shoot or a stem propagated by layering (see below).

LAYERING - A method of vegetative reproduction in which roots are induced to form along a shoot or a stem while it is still attached to the parent plant.

LEAFLET - One of the parts of a compound leaf.

LINEAR - Narrow and elongated.

LIP - The lower petal of an orchid flower, usually much larger than the others.

LOBED - Indented at the margins not more than half way to the center so that distinct parts appear.

MIDRIB - The central vein of a leaf.

NODE - That part of a stem from which the leaves or branches arise.

OPPOSITE - Two leaves at a node, one attached directly opposite the other on the stem.

ORBICULAR - More or less round.

OVATE - Outline of an egg, broader at the base.

PALMATE - Three or more divisions radiately lobed or arranged so as to seem to radiate from one point (resembling a hand).

PANICLE - A rebranching elongated and compound flower cluster (a branched raceme).

PARALLEL VEINED - Two or more smaller side veins on either side of and similar to the main vein.

PEDICEL - The stalk of an individual flower.

PEDUNCLE - A flower stalk or stem of an individual flower or the axis for a flower cluster or inflorescence.

PELTATE - Shield shaped.

PERENNIAL - An herbaceous non-woody plant which dies to the ground at the end of the growing season. The underground parts stay alive and produce new shoots the following season. May be short-lived or long-lived.

PERFOLIATE - Leaf blade completely surrounding the stem which appears to extend through the leaf.

PETAL - One of the units of a corolla—usually colored. May be separated or joined at the base.

PETIOLATE - Having a stalk or petiole.

PETIOLE - Stalklike part of a leaf attaching it to the stem.

PINNATE - Many leaflets arranged along sides of a common petiole.

PISTILLATE - A flower bearing only female organs (pistils), no stamens.

PUBESCENT - Covered in soft short hairs, downy.

RACEME - A flower cluster without branching where each flower is arranged singularly along the same stem, each flower on its own stalk, the lowest flower blooming first.

RARE SPECIES - Species that should be protected because of its scarcity.

RAY - Flat "petals" or irregular flowers (florets) that surround the disc flowers in a composite flower head—the showy part of a flower.

REGULAR FLOWER - A flower in which petals and/or sepals are arranged symetrically around the center.

ROSETTE - A circular cluster of basal leaves.

RUNNER - A stem that grows on the ground surface.

SCAPE - Flowering stem devoid of leaves and arising directly from the crown or root of the plant.

SCARIFICATION - Process used for seeds that have thick coats that are impervious to air and water. The seed coat must be damaged (i.e., nicked with sharp object) to make space to let elements in. Another method is to add seed to hot water, leaving until it has cooled.

SEPAL - Individual segment of a calyx—modified leaf near rim of flower.

SERRATE - Toothed like a saw along the margins.

SESSILE - Clasping, without a stalk, attached directly to a stem.

SHEATH - A tubular structure surrounding a part.

SHRUB - A woody plant that has several main stems arising from the base; usually smaller than a tree.

SIMPLE LEAF - Solitary leaf, one which is not divided into leaflets, edges may be lobed or entire.

SPADIX - Fleshy head or club shaped stalk crowded with numerous tiny blossoms.

SPATHE - Hooded or leaf like sheath that folds over on the top, usually covering a spadix.

SPIKE - Longer flower cluster with stalkless flowers arranged along the stem.

SPUR - A slender, usually hollow, projection from the base of a sepal, petal or fused corolla of certain flowers, as in larkspur.

STAMINATE - A flower bearing only male organs—stamens (no pistils).

STANDARD - The upper petal of a pea flower—the upright petal of an iris.

STIPULATE - Bearing stipules (see below).

STIPULE - A leafy appendage, usually paired, sometimes fused at the base of and on either side of some leaf petioles.

STRATIFICATION - Process used to break the dormancy of seed. Cold method—seal seed in plastic bag with slightly moistened sand or peat and store in refrigerator for specified period. Sow seed immediately when time expires. Seed can be sown in fall for spring germination. Warm method—seed and moistened peat in sealed plastic bag stored at warm temperature.

TERMINAL - Inflorescence at the tip of the main stem.

THREATENED SPECIES - A species likely to become endangered within the foreseeable future throughout all or part of its range or one legally designated threatened by Endangered Species Act.

TWO-LIPPED - Petals or sepals which are united to form a tube—may spread at the end into unequal upper and lower lips.

UMBEL - Flower cluster where flower stalks arise from same point in the stem, cluster having a round or flat top.

WHORL - Three or more leaves in a circle around the stem at the same level—not spiraled.

WING - Thin projecting membrane or flange or lateral (butterfly like) petal of a pea flower.

FLOWER INFLORESCENCE

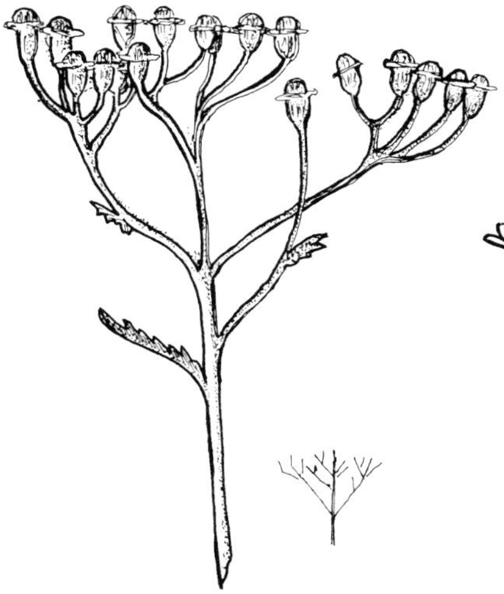

Corymb

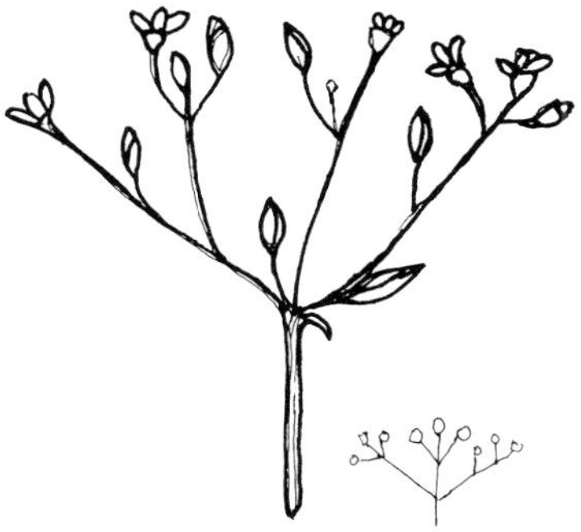

Cyme

Panicle

Raceme

Spadix and
Spathe

Umbel

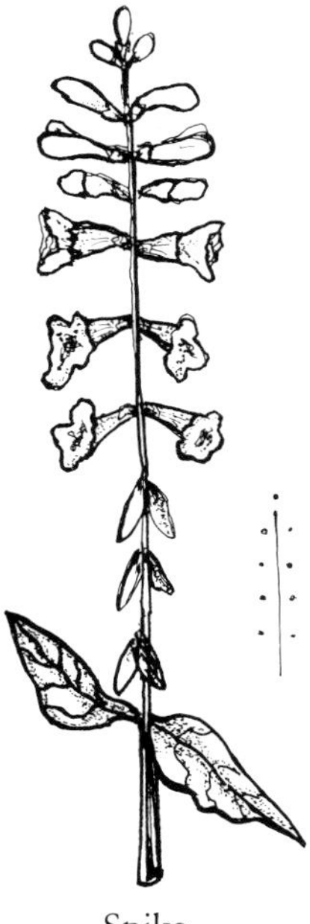

Spike

LEAF ARRANGEMENT
(Simple)

Alternate

Rosette

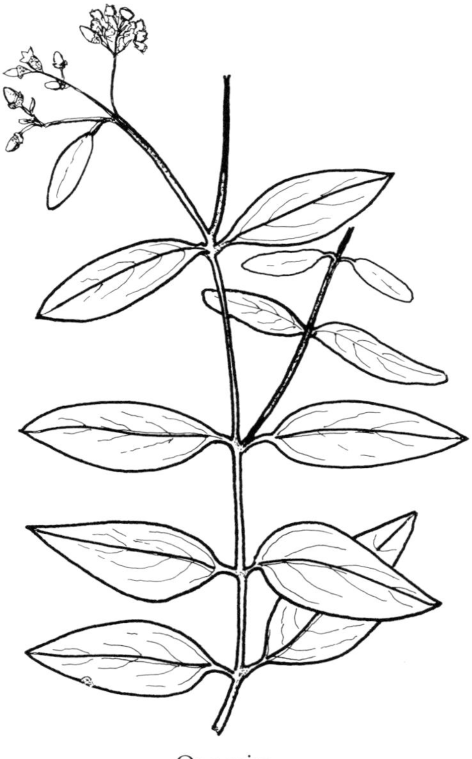

Opposite

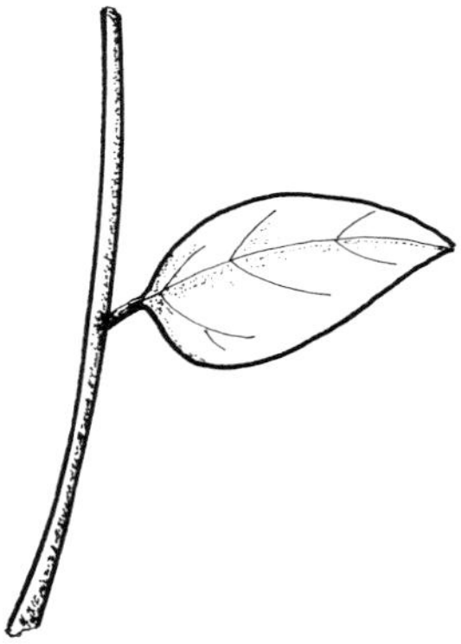

Simple

Whorl

LEAF ARRANGEMENT
(Compound)

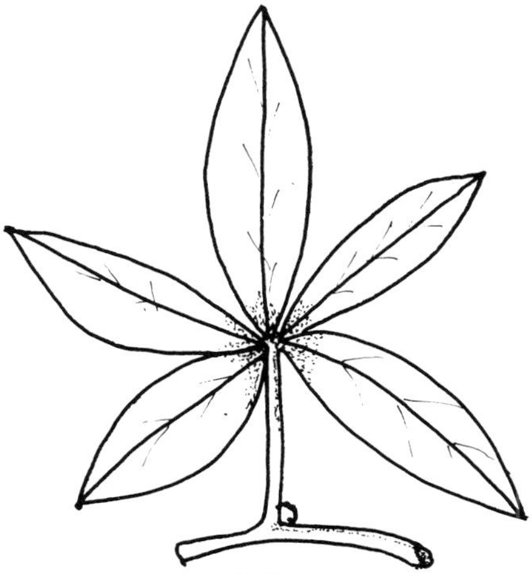

Palmate

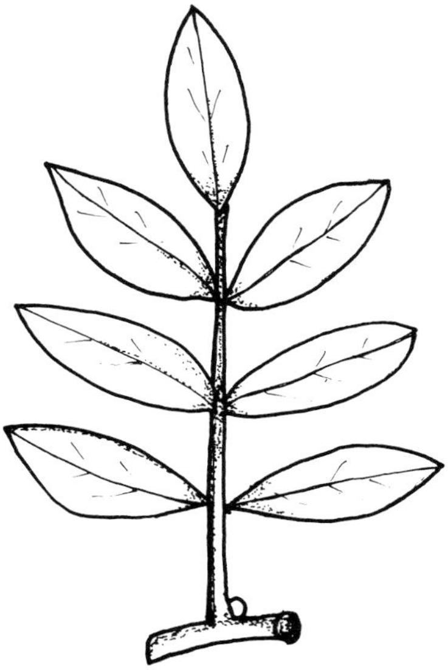

Pinnate

Bipinnate

LEAF SHAPE

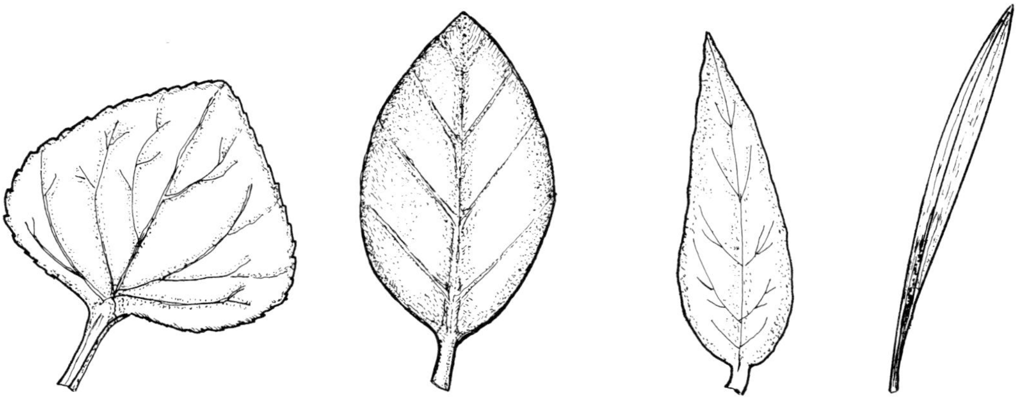

Deltoid Elliptic Lanceolate Linear

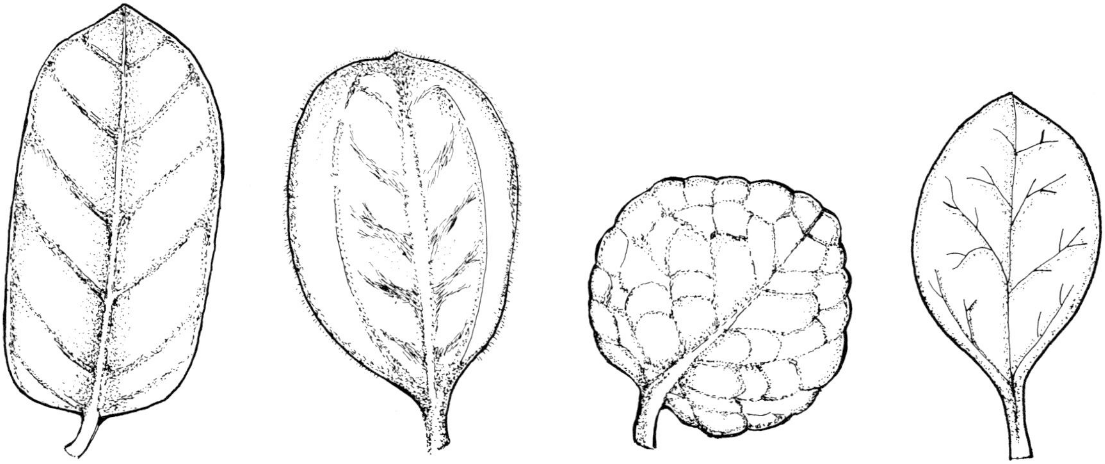

Oblong Obovate Orbicular Ovate

LEAF TIPS

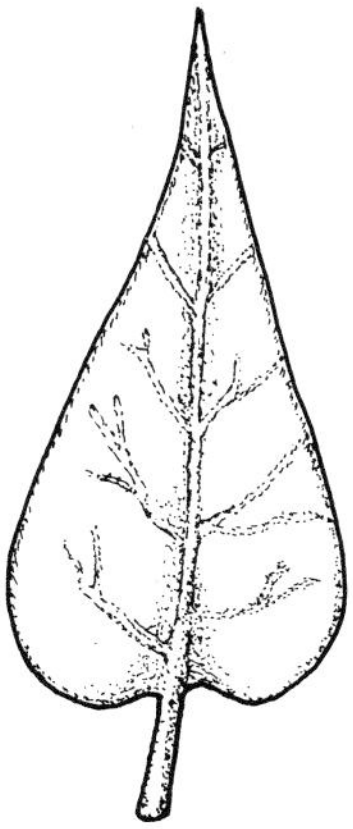

Accuminate

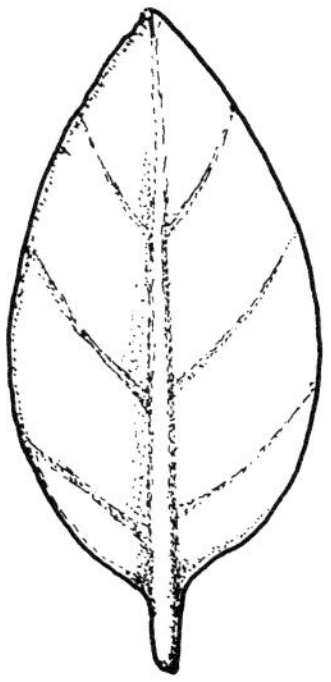

Acute

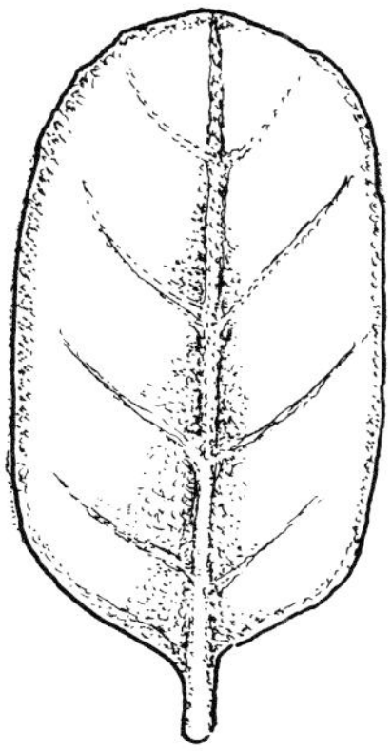

Obtuse

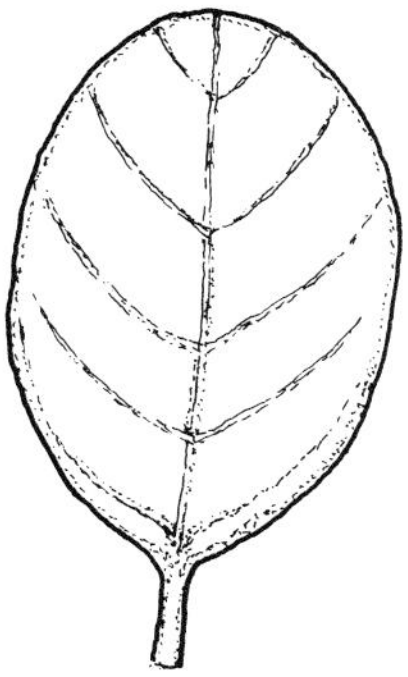

Rounded

LEAF BASES

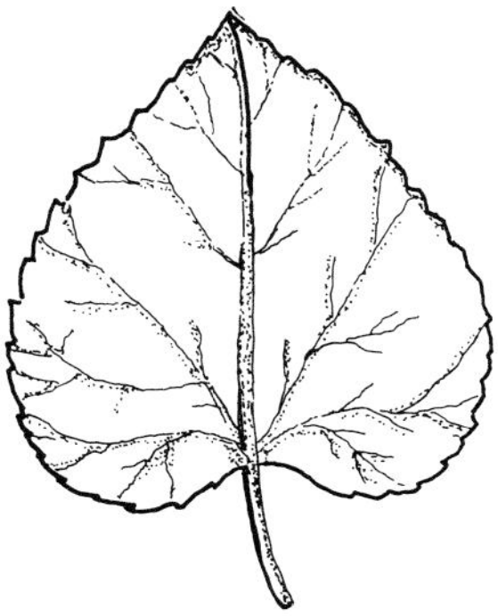

Cordate

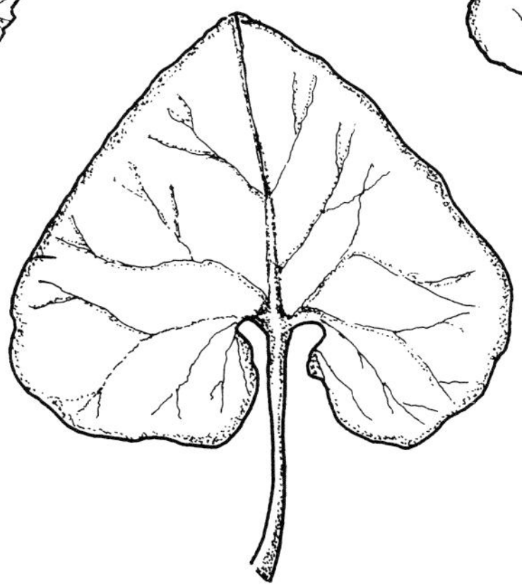

Eared

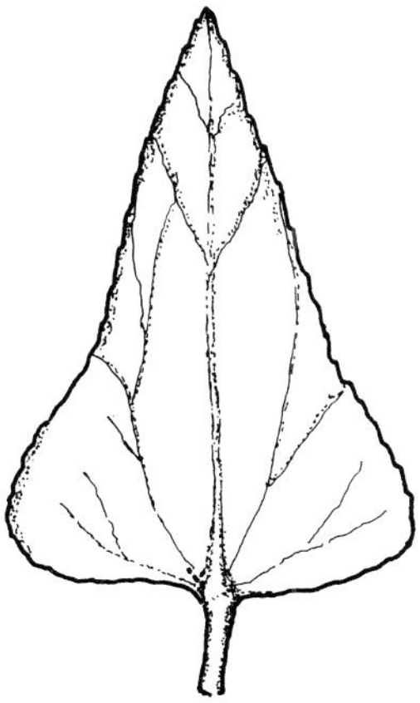

Hastate

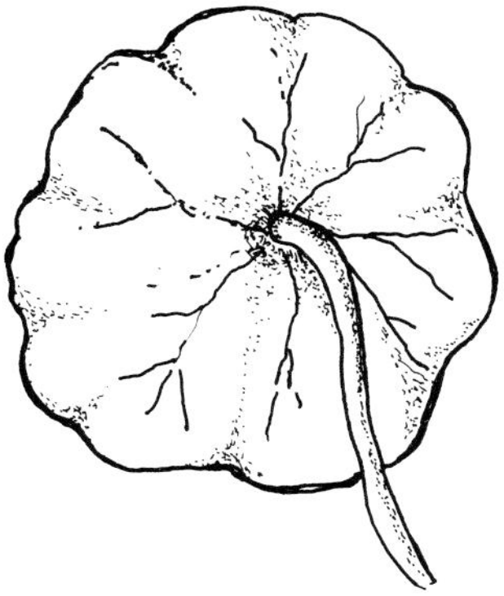

Peltate

LEAF MARGINS

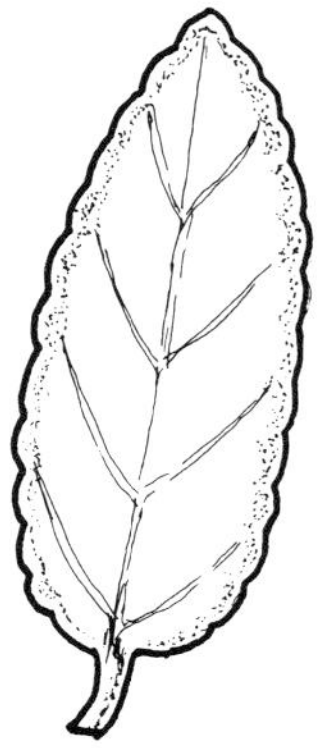

Crennate

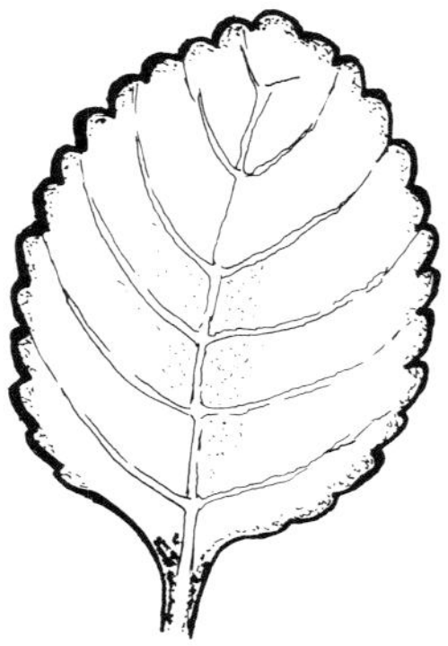

Dentate

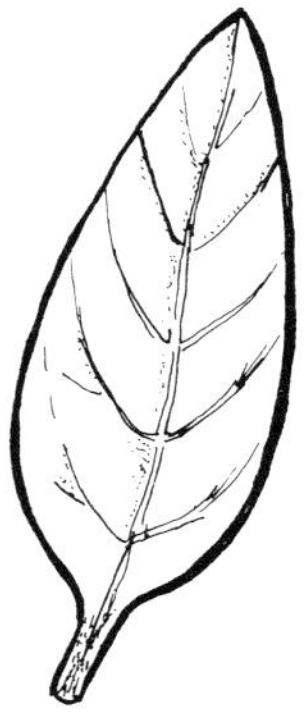

Entire

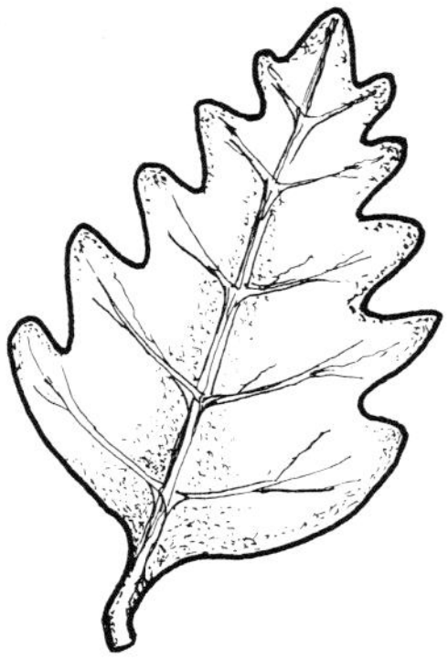

Lobed

Serrate

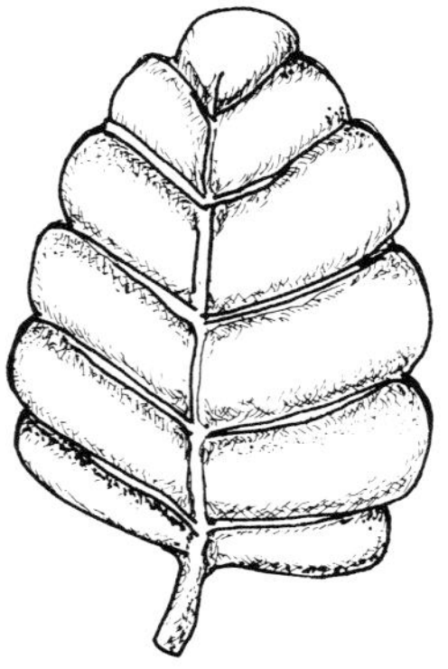

Undulate

LEAF ATTACHMENT

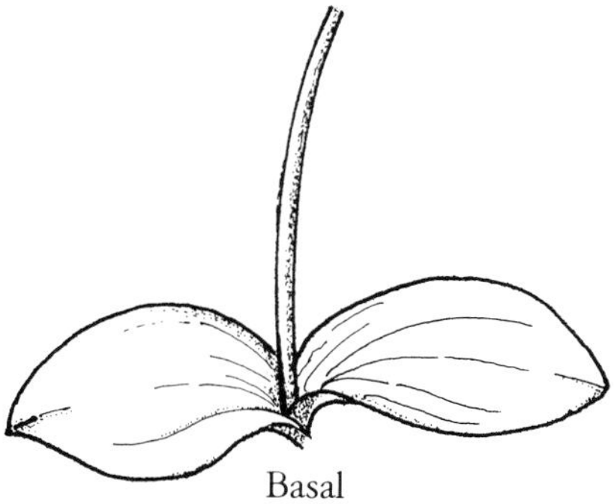

Basal

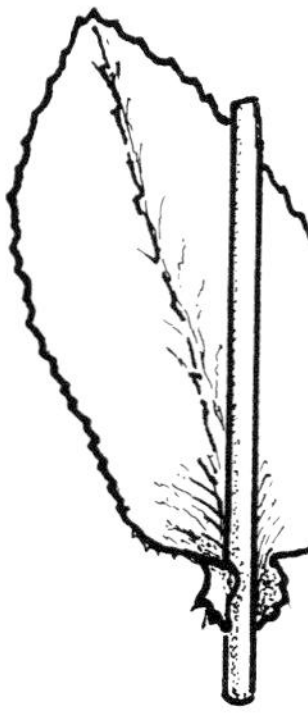

Clasping
or Sessile

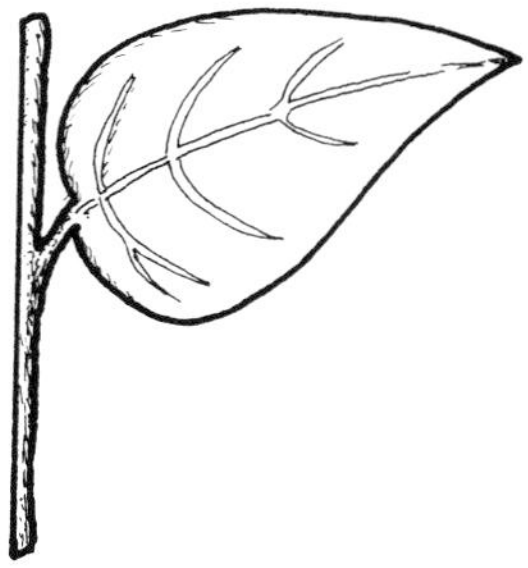

Petiolate

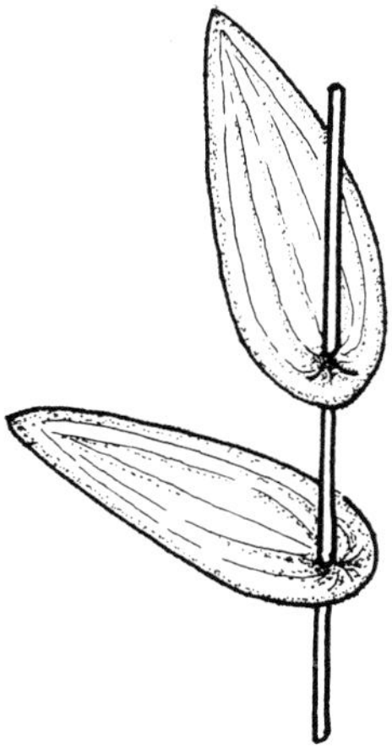

Perfoliate

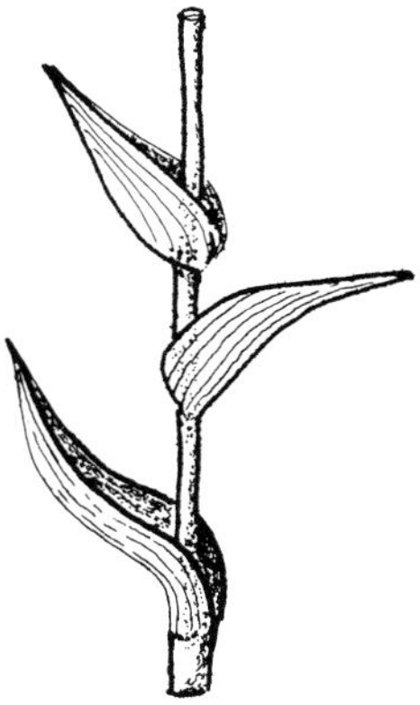

Sheathed

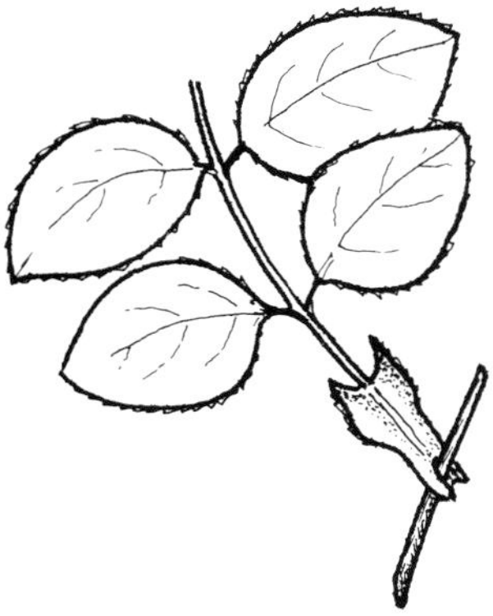

Stipulate

LOCATIONS IN GEORGIA WITH WILDFLOWER AND/OR WILD PLANT TRAILS OR GARDENS OPEN TO THE PUBLIC

(Admission fee may be charged)

Reed Bingham State Park
Rt. 2, P.O. Box 394
Adel, GA 31620
912-896-3551

The State Botanical Garden of Georgia
University of Georgia
3450 S. Milledge Avenue
Athens, GA 30605
Visitor Center: 706-542-6329

Atlanta Botanical Gardens
Piedmont Park at The Prado
P.O. Box 77246
Atlanta, GA 30357
404-876-5858

Atlanta Historical Society
3101 Andrews Drive, N.W.
Atlanta, GA 30305
404-261-1837

Fernbank Science Center
156 Heaton Park Drive
Atlanta, GA 30307
404-378-4311

Lullwater Conservation Garden
Lullwater Road
Atlanta, GA 30307

Vogel State Park
Route 1, Box 1230
Blairsville, GA 30512
706-745-2628

Cline's Garden
Waleska Highway
Canton, GA 30114
(Reservation required)

Red Top Mountain State Park
Cartersville, GA 31020
706-974-5184

Fort Mountain Park
Chatsworth, GA 30705
706-695-2621

Watson Mill Bridge State Park
Comer, GA 30629
706-783-5349

Amicalola Falls State Park
Star Route
Dawsonville, GA 30534
706-291-0766

DeKalb College Botanical Garden
DeKalb College, South Campus
3251 Panthersville Road
Decatur, GA 30034
404-244-5097

Stephen C. Foster State Park
Fargo, GA 31631
912-637-5274

Unicoi State Park
P.O. Box 256
Helen, GA 30545
706-878-2824

Dorset Trails
Mt. Vernon Church Road
Jackson, GA 30233

Sweetwater Creek Historic Park
P.O. Box 816
Mt. Vernon Road
Lithia Springs, GA 30057
404-944-1700

Providence Canyon State Park
Lumpkin, GA 31815
912-838-6202

Little Ocmulgee State Park
McRae, GA 31055
912-868-2832

Magnolia Springs State Park
Rt. 5, Box 488
Millen, GA 30442
912-982-1660

Black Rock Mountain State Park
Mountain City, GA 30562
706-746-2141

General Coffee State Park
Nicholls, GA 31554
912-384-7082

Cochran Mill Park
6875 Cochran Mill Road
Palmetto, GA 30268
404-463-4706

Callaway Gardens
Pine Mountain, GA 31822
404-663-2281, Ext. 154

Franklin D. Roosevelt State Park
Pine Mountain, GA 31822
404-663-4858

Marshall Forest
Rome Recreation Department
Rome, GA 30161
404-291-9766

Chattahoochee Nature Center
9135 Willeo Road
Roswell, GA
404-992-2055

Hard Labor Creek State Park
Rutledge, GA 30663
706-557-2863

Skidaway Island State Park
Savannah, GA 31406
912-598-0393

Crooked River State Park
3092 Spur 40
St. Marys, GA 31558
912-882-5256

Panola Mountain Conservation Park
2600-A Hwy. 155 S.
Stockbridge, GA 30281
404-474-2912

Georgia's Stone Mountain Park
Stone Mountain, GA 30087
404-498-5702

Okefenokee Swamp Park
State Route 117
Waycross, GA 31501
912-283-0583

PLACES TO BUY WILDFLOWER SEEDS, PLANTS, SHRUBS AND OTHER WILD PLANTS

This listing is not intended to be an endorsement but is for information as to sources where seeds and/or plants may be available. Some companies have a nominal charge for a catalog.

GEORGIA

The State Botanical Garden of Georgia
University of Georgia
3450 S. Milledge Avenue
Athens, GA 30605
Visitor Center 706-542-6329
Spring and Fall Plant Sales

Atlanta Botanical Gardens
Piedmont Park at The Prado
P.O. Box 77242
Atlanta, GA 30357
404-876-5858
Spring and Fall Plant Sales

H. G. Hastings
P.O. Box 4274
Atlanta, GA 30302
800-334-1771

Pennington Enterprises
P.O. Box 290
Atlanta Highway
Madison, GA 30650
706-342-1234

Thomasville Nurseries, Inc.
P.O. Box 7
Thomasville, GA 31799
912-226-5568
Wild Azaleas

Transplant Nursery
Parkerton Road
Lavonia, GA 30553
706-356-8947

NORTH CAROLINA

Huffman's Native Plants
U.S. Highway 441, South
P.O. Box 39
Otto, NC 28763
704-524-7446

Gardens of the Blue Ridge
E. P. Robbins, Nurseryman
P.O. Box 10
Pineola, NC 38662

Lamtree Farm
Rt. 1, Box 162
Warrenville, NC 28693
919-385-6144

SOUTH CAROLINA

Wayside Gardens
Hodges, SC 29695-0001
800-845-1124

Park Seed Co.
Cokesbury Road, Highway 254
Greenwood, SC 29647-0001
800-845-3366

Woodlanders
1128 Colleton Ave.
Aiken, SC 29801

TENNESSEE

Native Gardens
Rt. 1, Box 494
Greenback, TN 37742
615-856-3350

Natural Gardens
4804 Shell Lane
Knoxville, TN 37918

Sunlight Gardens, Inc.
Rt. 3, Box 286-B
Loudon, TN 37774

SELECTED BIBLIOGRAPHY

Art, Henry. *A Garden of Wildflowers: 101 Native Species & How to Grow Them*. Storey Communication, Inc., Pownal, Vt., 1986

Austin, Richard L. *Wild Gardening*. Simon and Schuster, New York. 1986

Baines, Chris. *How to Make a Wildlife Garden*. Elm Tree Books, London, 1985.

Brooklyn Botanic Garden. *Handbook on Gardening with Wildflowers*. Vol. 18 (1), Brooklyn, N.Y., 1962

Brown, Lauren. *Weeds in Winter*. W. W. Norton & Company, New York, 1976.

Bruce, Hal. *How to Grow Wildflowers & Wild Shrubs & Trees in Your Own Garden*. Alfred Knopt, New York, 1976.

Crawford, Barrie E. *For the Love of Wildflowers*. Buckeye Press, Columbus, Ga., 1985.

Crockett, James E. Oliver & the editors of Time-Life Books. *Wildflower Gardening*. Time-Life Encyclopedia of Gardening, Vol. 14, Time-Life Books, Alexandria, Va., 1977.

Cronquist, Arthur. *Vascular Flora of the Southeastern United States*. The University of North Carolina Press, Chapel Hill, N. C., 1980.

Damrosch, Barbara. *Theme Gardens*. Workman Publishing, New York, 1982.

Dean, Blanche; Mason, Amy & Thomas, Joab. *Wildflowers of Alabama & Adjoining States*. The University of Alabama Press, University, Ala., 1973.

Diekelmann, John & Schuster, R., *Natural Landscaping, Designing with Native Plant Communities*. McGraw-Hill, New York, 1982.

Dorman, Caroline. *Flowers Native to the Deep South*. Clairtor's Book Store, Baton Rouge, La., 1958.

Duncan, Wilbur and Foote, Leonard. *Wildflowers of the Southeastern United States*. The University of Georgia Press, Athens, Ga., 1975.

Fendig, Gladys and Stewart, Esther. *Native Flora of the Golden Isles*. Sentinel Print, Jesup, Ga. 1970.

Gottehrer, Dean. *Natural Landscaping*. McGraw-Hill, New York, 1982.

Klaber, Doretta. *Violets of the United States*. A. S. Barnes and Company. Cranbury, N. J., 1976

Martin, Laura. *Southern Wildflowers*. Longstreet Press, Marietta, Ga., 1989.

Martin, Laura. *The Wildflower Meadow Book*. East Woods Press Book, Charlotte, N. C., 1986.

McHarg, Ian. *Design with Nature*. Natural History Press, Garden City, N. Y., 1971.

McKinley, Michael, *How to Attract Birds*. Ortho Press, San Francisco, Ca. 1983.

Naveh, Zev & Liberman, Arthur. *Landscape Ecology. Theory & Application* Springer-Verlag, New York, 1984.

Niering, William A; Olmstead, Nancy C. *The Audubon Society Field Guide to North American Wildflowers - Eastern Region*. Alfred A. Knopf, New York, 1979.

Penn, Cordelia. *Landscaping with Native Plants.* John Blair, Winston-Salem, N. C., 1982.

Peterson, Roger Tory; McKenny, Margaret. *A Field Guide to Wildflowers*, Houghton Mifflin Company, Boston, Mass. 1968.

Phillips, Harry. *Growing and Propagating Wild Flowers.* University of North Carolina Press, Chapel Hill, N. C., 1985.

Pond, Barbara. *A Sampler of Wayside Herbs.* Greenwich House, New York, 1974.

Smith, Arlo. *A Guide to Wildflowers of the Mid-South.* Memphis State University Press, Memphis, Tenn., 1979.

Smyzer, Carol. *Nature's Design.* Rodale Press, Emmaus, Pa., 1981.

Snyder, Lloyd H., Jr.,; Bruce, James G., *Field Guide to the Ferns & Other Pteridrophytes of Georgia.* The University of Georgia Press, Athens, Ga. 1986.

Steffek, Edwin. *The New Wild Flowers and How to Grow Them.* Timber Press, Portland, Or. 1983.

Stevenson, Violet. *The Wild Garden: Making Natural Gardens Using Wild & Native Plants.* Penguin Press, New York, 1985.

Stupka, Arthur. *Trees, Shrubs & Woody Vines of Great Smoky Mountains National Park.* The University of Tennessee Press, Knoxville, Tenn. 1964.

Tekulsky, Matthew. *The Butterfly Garden.* The Harvard Common Press, Boston, Mass. 1985.

Wilson, William H. W., *Landscaping With Wildflowers and Native Plants* Ortho Books, San Francisco, Ca., 1984.

Young, James & Cheryl. *Collecting, Processing & Germinating Seeds of Wildland Plants.* Timber Press, Portland, Or., 1986.

INDEX

H

I

T

X - Y

Z

NOTES:

NOTES:

NOTES:

NOTES: